IronFit®'s
Marathons After 40

Also by **Don Fink** *and* **Melanie Fink**

Be Iron Fit, Third Edition
IronFit® Secrets for Half Iron-Distance Triathlon Success
IronFit® Triathlon Training for Women
IronFit® Strength Training and Nutrition for Endurance Athletes

IronFit®'s
Marathons After 40

SMARTER TRAINING FOR THE AGELESS ATHLETE

DON FINK AND **MELANIE FINK**

Guilford, Connecticut

An imprint of Globe Pequot

Distributed by NATIONAL BOOK NETWORK

Copyright © 2010 and 2017 Don Fink and Melanie Fink
IronFit® is a registered trademark of Don Fink, all rights reserved.
All exercise photos featuring Yvonne Hernandez are provided courtesy of Debra Trebitz.

British Library Cataloguing in Publication Information available

Library of Congress Cataloging-in-Publication Data available

ISBN 978-1-4930-2687-6 (paperback)
ISBN 978-1-4930-2688-3 (e-book)

♾™ The paper used in this publication meets the minimum requirements of American National Standard for Information Sciences—Permanence of Paper for Printed Library Materials, ANSI/NISO Z39.48-1992.

The programs in this book are designed for athletes with either a high level of fitness or the physiology to attain a high level of fitness. Readers should consult a physician before beginning any of the workouts suggested herein. If you experience any pain or difficulty with these exercises, stop and consult your health care provider.

To our loving parents,
Claire and Richard and Esther and Martin

» CONTENTS

» INTRODUCTION

Seven years . . . wow!

It's amazing to us that it's been more than seven years since an earlier version of this book, *Mastering the Marathon*, was published. It has been an exciting time for the sport, which continues to skyrocket in popularity worldwide. The entire marathon experience has continued to get better and better.

As we have traveled the world over this time, we have been blessed to see so many wonderful races and meet so many truly inspiring people who share our passion.

We have been working with hundreds and hundreds of athletes over the last seven years, and we have continued to improve upon our coaching methods and approaches. We have successfully found ways to make our training even more efficient and beneficial.

Because of this, the time has now come to offer a new generation of Masters Marathon training programs, including all of these advancements and improvements. So, yes, as successful as the original programs were, the five new marathon training programs in this book are even better. In fact, not only are they better, but they are more fun too.

We are also excited about many new additions to this edition. We have a new chapter focusing on the half marathon with three twelve-week training programs and tips and guidance on how to maximize your performance in this popular distance. We have also included a new chapter specifically geared to triathletes who want to maximize their marathon performance within an Iron-Distance triathlon. And, most excitingly, we have included all-new state-of-the-art functional strength and core training, dynamic warm-up, and stretching programs.

Now it's your turn. Since you're reading this book, we know that you have exciting goals you want to accomplish in road racing. Perhaps you are still deciding if you want to take the marathon or half marathon plunge, or perhaps you already have completed the marathon or half marathon but are ready to improve your times and take your performances to the next level. Either way, you have come to the right place. Let your journey begin!

If you are forty years or older and would like to run faster marathons or take on the marathon challenge for the first time, this book is for you.

The American marathon boom that started in the 1970s is alive and well and growing every year. In the late 1970s about 25,000 Americans attempted a marathon annually; by the year 2010, this number exceeded 500,000.

Athletes of all ages view the marathon as a wonderful lifetime accomplishment. Some may consider it a goal to accomplish just once, while others see it as a recurring challenge. Nowhere is this truer than for those forty and older. This enormous segment of the population is especially keen on the marathon experience.

Have you been running for many years, but found that you are no longer improving like you once did? That the training methods you used to follow successfully when you were younger no longer seem to work? What's more, the more you try to make them work, the more injured and discouraged you become . . . pushing your goals farther out of reach. If so, you can benefit from a new training approach, specifically targeted to the more mature athlete. This book is written for you.

Or are you newer to the sport? You picked it up later in life, found it to be challenging and rewarding, but the methods you found online or in books don't seem to work for you. You notice that the programs you read about do not even differentiate among ages, let alone between veterans and first-timers. The program for a twenty-year-old is the same as for a sixty-year-old. You know that can't be right. You realize there must be a more sensible and effective way for the mature athlete to achieve his or her goals. This book is written for you as well.

I have coached many athletes who completed their first marathon after forty years of age; others who qualified for the Boston Marathon for the first time after forty; others who broke 3 hours for the first time after turning forty; and yes, even some who broke 2:50 for the first time after turning forty. This book includes the very same training principles and approaches that can help you achieve this same success.

Finally, some of you may not even be sure you want to run a marathon, but would like to learn how to get in better shape and . . . who knows . . . maybe try a 5K or 10K sometime in the future. This book is for you as well.

I will show you how there exist essentially three key weekly workouts to be included in your routine in order to improve your marathon. I call these workouts the "Three Magic Bullets." I will describe each one in detail, explain what it does and how it works and, most importantly, how to build it into your training program. I will also show you how you can even estimate what your marathon time will be based on your progress in these three workouts.

I will also present the exact type of training an athlete should do on the days when he is not engaged in one of the Magic Bullet workouts. This will differ depending on the athlete's injury history and experience. These sessions may very well include additional runs, but the important thing to know is that they may not; they may instead include other types of training. That's right! You can improve your marathon performance with as few as three runs per week.

How can this be? The simple answer is effective cross-training. The additional "runs" don't actually need to be runs. This is a welcome revelation for those with a history of running injuries. But the truth for all runners is that if you know how to build the proper type of cross-training around the three key weekly training sessions, you can achieve your marathon goals with as few as three runs per week. This book will show you how.

Not only will I present what the key workouts and cross-training sessions are, how to correctly complete them, and how to build them into an effective training program, but I will also offer several sample training programs to choose from. Readers can quickly determine which one best fits their situation and immediately put it to work for them.

Besides the key training plans and cross-training workouts, this book also includes my cutting edge core and functional-strength training programs, which perfectly complement these training plans and provide the forty-plus athlete with the strength foundation necessary to take his or her marathon performance to an entirely new level. Is strength and core training important for forty-plus athletes? You bet it is. In fact, it's far more important as we get older. I'll present my ideas for warm-up, cooldown, and stretching routines too.

I will additionally show you how to select the optimal tune-up races to build into your running and racing schedule. Obviously running additional 5K, 10K, and half marathon races can be helpful in preparing for the marathon, but how many of these races should an athlete do, and what is the best time to schedule them relative to the date of your marathon in order to get the best results?

We will look at the most common marathon training and racing mistakes and how to avoid them. Many times marathon training can be counterintuitive—something that seems to make perfect sense is actually a mistake that will lead to ineffective training or even injury. I'll present the most common mistakes associated with both training and racing and help you to steer clear of them.

While many athletes hate to hear this, the truth is that leaner is usually faster. Our body weight is an important determiner of our marathon performance. Our leanest healthy body weight is usually our fastest body weight. It is surprising how many marathoners ignore this important element for success. I will present tips and methods for maintaining a healthy, lean, and fast body weight. The strength and nutritional plans included in this book will have you looking and feeling your fittest ever.

I will also present my highly effective race strategies and mental approaches for getting the absolute most from your fitness level. Fueling and hydration strategies are included to keep you energized and hydrated throughout your training and racing.

Our marathon careers don't end at forty. In fact, not only are fast marathons still possible, but the potential for enjoying the sport and our fitness is greater than ever. All it takes is a mind open to trying some new approaches and a fresh new outlook. One of the most important aspects to keep in mind is that my training programs, action steps, and tips are fun. This is not some grinding "no pain, no gain" training routine to be feared. All of the workouts are challenging, motivating, and rewarding. I will not present a lot of scientific discussion, technical talk, and complicated formulas to figure out—just straight talk and a clear path to achieving your marathon goals. This, combined with the dedication and drive I suspect you already have, will have you achieving performance levels you never thought possible at your age. So, turn the page and let's get started!

» Three Magic Bullets

To give anything less than your best is to sacrifice the gift. —STEVE PREFONTAINE

The Three Magic Bullets are simply three key workouts that will help you achieve your marathon dreams and give you the racing results you want.

So many athletes are out there focusing on quantity over quality. Their training is filled with purposeless runs, done merely to rack up volume. One day just sort of morphs into the next, and there is no real plan or purpose to most of the runs in their week. This "more is always better" approach is extremely inefficient training and in the long run leads to performance stagnation, boredom, and possibly even injury. This is especially true for the forty-plus athlete.

What if we told you there are three "magic bullet" workouts that, if arranged properly within a sixteen-week marathon training program, will do more than anything else to get you to your marathon goal? The great news is that these Three Magic Bullets workouts are real. What's even more exciting is that these three workouts are fun to do and add great variety to marathon training. These three training sessions should form the core of any marathon training program for the forty-plus athlete.

While the Three Magic Bullets sessions should be a part of just about any marathoner's plan, they are especially important for the forty-plus marathoner. The typically busy over-forty marathoner doesn't have the luxury of being able to waste time and effort on a lot of junk training. He needs to train efficiently and maximize the training benefit of each and every training moment. The three key workouts, built properly into an overall plan, will do exactly that.

Many marathoners, especially younger ones, do a lot of higher-volume training, and much of it is not completely focused. In a successful training plan, each workout should have a specific purpose and should work in harmony with the other workouts in the marathoner's training week.

We have developed and fine-tuned our approach to the Three Magic Bullets over decades of working with successful marathoners. Each workout has a specific purpose, and together they are a powerful combination for a fast marathon. Together they provide truly synergistic training, where the combined training benefit of the three workouts is greater than the sum of the individual workout's training benefits.

Adriana Nelson, world-class marathoner
101 Degrees West

As amazing as the Three Magic Bullets are, their training benefit can be increased even more when combined with the proper complement of other workouts. We will present each of these complementary workout strategies in this book, but the Three Magic Bullets sessions form the heart of our approach to fast marathoning.

This chapter will explain each of the Three Magic Bullets workouts in detail and how to get the most out of them. Future chapters will discuss the other workouts and activities that need to be built around the three key workouts in order to achieve your optimal marathon training program. Later in the chapter, we will unveil why the Three Magic Bullets workouts are "magic." So stay tuned; you are going to love it.

THE THREE MAGIC BULLETS (TMBs)

- Marathon Pacing Session

- Long Run

- Higher-Intensity Repeats

≫ Marathon Pacing Session

The marathon is the ultimate pacing race. We will talk more about pacing strategies in Chapter 11, but in general, if you can hit just the right pace for you, you will maximize your marathon performance. On the other hand, if you miss your proper pace, you may be bound for a miserable and unforgiving 26.2 miles.

The most common mistake in all endurance races is going out too fast. It's easy to do, and we have made this mistake ourselves over the years. As much as this applies to virtually all distances and all types of endurance races, it is never truer than in the marathon distance. There is nothing as uncomfortable and miserable as the feeling you get in the last 10K of a marathon after having gone out too fast in the first 10K.

Coaches and athletes alike often joke about the "4–1" rule. There are various interpretations of this rule, but the one we find most accurate is the following: For every 1 second per mile faster than optimal pace you run in the first 10K of the marathon, you will give back up to 4 seconds per mile in the final 10K of the marathon. This means that if your optimal race pace was 7:00 minutes per mile and instead you averaged 6:45 minutes per mile (15 seconds per mile faster than your optimal race pace) in the first 10K, then you are likely to find you can only average as slow as 8:00 minutes per mile (60 seconds per mile slower than your optimal race pace) in the final 10K. The ratio between 60 seconds and 15 seconds is 4 to 1.

It's amazing how often this ratio holds true. In analyzing the racing results of hundreds of athletes over the years, we have seen this phenomenon repeat itself time and time again. An athlete trains for a very specific pace throughout his training cycle. Then he succumbs to that euphoric feeling athletes sometimes get at the beginning of a race, and in an instant throws out the pacing plan and decides to start clicking off the miles at a faster pace.

There are many reasons for the euphoric feeling at the start of a marathon. It's due partially to the fact that athletes are well rested and tapered for the race, so energy levels are especially high. It's due also to the thrill and excitement of competition, spectators, and the event itself. But more often than not, the athlete who goes out 15 seconds per mile faster than optimal pace will "hit the wall" somewhere around 20 miles into the marathon and, as noted above, his pace over the final 10K will average closer to 60 seconds per mile slower than planned.

As we will discuss further in this chapter and under "Pacing" in Chapter 11 and "Five Common Racing Mistakes to Avoid" in Chapter 12, trying to "bank time" in the early stages is not a good marathon strategy.

The Marathon Pacing Session is a key workout because it teaches us physically and mentally to run at our target pace and to do it as evenly and as efficiently as possible. Not only do we physically and mentally "lock it in," but by repeating these sessions week after week, we become comfortable with the pace and find that we can relax more while holding the pace.

Following is an example of a 75-minute Marathon Pacing Session:

- Start with 40 minutes at a moderate pace of 30 to 60 seconds per mile slower than your Target Marathon Pace.

- For the next 30 minutes, increase your pace to your Target Marathon Pace.

- Finish with a moderate 5 minutes at 30 to 60 seconds slower than Target Marathon Pace.

As seen in the above example, the pacing portion of the Marathon Pacing Session is placed toward the end of the total run time. The athlete begins the workout by running at a moderate pace for the first 40 minutes, then increases his pace to his Target Marathon Pace for the next 30 minutes, then returns to a moderate pace for the final 5 minutes.

Typically we like to start these weekly sessions in the eighth week of a sixteen-week marathon preparation phase, with an insert of 30 minutes at Target Marathon Pace. Then we increase the insert by 10 minutes per week to a peak of 80 minutes, depending on the experience level of the athlete, prior to beginning a three-week taper leading up to the race.

Following is one example of how these sessions may be structured starting in the eighth week of a sixteen-week marathon preparation phase. The actual marathon training plans in Chapter 5 will provide more examples and also show how this one key session can effectively be built into an overall marathon training program.

WEEK NUMBER	LENGTH OF TOTAL RUN	LENGTH OF PACING PORTION
8	75 minutes	30 minutes
9	75	40
10	90	50
11	90	60
12	90	70
13	90	80
14	75	40
15	60	20
16	Marathon	

The sessions in the above example start out in the eighth week of the sixteen-week marathon training plan at 75 minutes and increase to 90 minutes in the tenth week. With two weeks to go, they taper to 75 minutes and then to 60 minutes with one week before race day.

Each of these sessions start out in Z2 (Heart Rate Zone 2). We will fully explain Heart Rate Zones in Chapter 5, but for now let's define Z2 as a fairly moderate effort, about 75–85 percent of maximum heart rate.

At a designated point in the run, we increase our pace to our Target Marathon Pace and hold it steady and evenly for the designated period. As seen in the example, the length of this pacing portion increases by 10 minutes each week until it peaks at 80 minutes, at which point it begins to taper down in anticipation of the race.

Here's a little warning: We said the three key workouts were magic, but we didn't say they were easy. The Marathon Pacing Session tends to be a very challenging workout—rewarding and highly effective, but challenging.

Later we will discuss how to determine your optimal Target Marathon Pace, but for most athletes, their target pace will have them in, or close to, an 86–89 percent range of maximum heart rate (Z3: Heart Rate Zone 3) for most of their Marathon Pacing Session. We will discuss pacing strategies in greater detail in Chapter 11, but generally our suggestion is to set your Target Marathon Pace at 5 to 7 seconds per mile faster than the actual pace necessary to achieve your marathon goal. This is not an attempt to "bank" a large amount of time, but instead to provide just a slight cushion of 2 to 3 minutes under your marathon time goal. For example, if your goal is to go under 3 hours for the marathon, which is about a 6:51-minute-per-mile pace, you may want to set your Target Marathon Pace at 6:45 minutes per mile, thus building in a small cushion of about 6 seconds per mile, or about 3 minutes for the entire race.

Once you build the pacing portion up to 80 minutes, it becomes pretty tough to maintain an effort in or close to the 86–89 percent of maximum heart-rate range. But there is no workout that will feel more rewarding or provide you with more pre-race confidence.

Of the Three Magic Bullets sessions (TMBs), this is the only one that does not have a cross-training substitution option. The workout can be done on a track, a measured course, or a treadmill, but it needs to be a run. We will discuss cross-training in more detail in Chapter 3, "Free Running Miles."

» Long Run

The second of the TMB workouts is the Long Run. This workout is all about building endurance for the marathon. If you want to successfully race long, you need to properly train long. The benefits of the Long Run are numerous:

- Builds the aerobic system

- Prepares the body for the physical stress of running long

- Provides an opportunity to practice fueling and hydrating properly

- Prepares the athlete for the mental stress of running long

The most common mistake you see in marathon preparation programs is too many Long Runs. In fact, some athletes do nothing but Long Runs to prepare. This is an inefficient approach and can be risky, especially for the over-forty athlete.

Long Runs should be completed at a pace of about 30 to 60 seconds per mile slower than the athlete's Target Marathon Pace. This usually equates to a Z1 to Z2 Heart Rate Zone. If your pace is closer to 30 seconds per mile slower than Target Marathon Pace, you are likely to be in Z2 (75–85 percent of maximum heart rate). If your pace is closer to 60 seconds per mile slower than Target Marathon Pace, you are likely to be in Z1 (65–74 percent of maximum heart rate). While these runs are generally more beneficial when completed in Z2, there is still good training benefit in Z1.

Many athletes run their Long Runs at too fast a pace. This of course stems from the "more is always better" training philosophy. If 30 seconds slower per mile is good, then 15 seconds slower per mile must be even better. But this is not true. The result is less-effective training, which diminishes the combined benefit of the Three Magic Bullets. Do not confuse this run with the Marathon Pacing Session. It has a different purpose, and if an athlete runs these sessions too fast, he is unlikely to maximize his performance on race day.

As you will see in the marathon training plans presented in Chapter 5, we suggest building up your Long Runs very gradually.

Once the Long Run reaches its longest duration, the pattern then becomes one of alternating "long and longer" every other week. For example, if the longest run is 3 hours, we will not move into the peak training weeks and merely run 3-hour Long Runs every week back to back. The body typically cannot absorb the benefits of 3-hour runs in several consecutive weeks. Instead, once we reach 3 hours, we will alternate our Long Runs for a few weeks with a pattern of a 3-hour run this week, then a 2.5-hour run next week, then a 3-hour run the following week, etc., before eventually transitioning into our taper. This also allows the body to fully absorb the benefits of Long Runs while reducing the risk of injury.

All of the Long Runs start out by building in a gradual pattern until they reach their peak duration. Once at their peak, Long Runs then convert to a "long and longer" alternating pattern for the biggest training weeks, before transitioning into the three-week taper prior to the marathon.

How long should the Long Run build to? Long Runs should generally be no longer than the lesser of 22 miles or 3.5 hours. The risk of becoming either injured or overly rundown becomes too great once the Long Run goes beyond 22 miles or 3.5 hours. So, for the vast majority of athletes, the lesser of 22 miles or 3.5 hours is optimal.

Typically the number of an athlete's longest runs (the lesser of 22 miles or 3.5 hours) are limited to three or four per marathon training cycle. This is because the Long Run is definitely a workout that can be overdone. Three or four runs at our longest training distance or time is all we need; any more than that increases the risk of injury. We want to make sure we do the proper number of Long Runs and place them optimally among our other training sessions.

Another way to reduce the risk of injury is through cross-training. In Chapters 3 and 5 we will discuss various cross-training approaches for the Long Run.

» Higher-Intensity Repeats

The third of the TMBs is the Higher-Intensity Repeat sessions. These are simply repeat drills done at a high level of effort with an easy timed recovery jog in between. Traditionally these are done on a track and are completed at 90–95 percent of maximum heart rate (74: Heart Rate Zone 4). Many athletes refer to these types of training sessions as "intervals." The name is a little misleading, however, because the "interval" portion of the session actually refers to the easy recovery jogs between the Higher-Intensity Repeat portions.

Following are some basic examples of Higher-Intensity Repeat sessions:

Example of a Short Repeat Session

- 1-mile easy warm-up jog

- 12 x 400 meters at 90–95 percent of maximum heart rate with an easy 200-meter recovery jog between each repeat

- 1-mile easy cooldown jog

Example of a Long Repeat Session

- 1-mile easy warm-up jog

- 4 x 1,600 meters at 90–95 percent of maximum heart rate with an easy 400-meter recovery jog between each repeat

- 1-mile easy cooldown jog

Your pacing on the repeats is important. Typically we suggest you do Short Repeats (800 meters or less) at about your 5K race pace and Long Repeats (1,600 meters or more) at about your 10K race pace. Both of these paces will probably put most athletes in, or close to, 90–95 percent of maximum heart rate. So if our fastest 5K and 10K are 21:45 and 45 minutes, respectively, then our Short Repeat and Long Repeat paces will be approximately 7:00 minutes per mile and 7:15 minutes per mile, respectively.

In general, all Higher-Intensity Repeats should be completed at a pace at least 30 seconds per mile faster than an athlete's Target Marathon Pace. If an athlete finds he cannot do this, it is an indication that the marathon goal he has set for himself may be unreasonable at this point in his development.

The best way to get accurate distance measurements is to run on a 400-meter track, but there can be disadvantages to running on a track—especially for the forty-plus athlete. Even if the track has a relatively soft surface, excessive turning can lead to injury. Keep this in mind and use caution. For most over-forty athletes, it's best to use the track in moderation.

Another option for Higher-Intensity Repeats is to get off the track and either use GPS or base the repeats on time instead of distance. Timed workouts can be done virtually anywhere, including the softer surface of a treadmill.

Following are examples of a timed approach for both Short and Long Repeat sessions:

Example of Short Repeat Session

- 10-minute easy warm-up jog

- 12 x 2 minutes at 90–95 percent of maximum heart rate with an easy 1-minute recovery jog between each repeat

- 10-minute easy cooldown jog

Example of Long Repeat Session

- 10-minute easy warm-up jog

- 4 x 7.5 minutes at 90–95 percent of maximum heart rate with an easy 3.5-minute jog between each repeat

- 10-minute easy cooldown jog

Typically we will design these sessions in a progression format, as you will see in the marathon training programs in Chapter 5. We will start with shorter repeats, such as 400 meters, and then build gradually in duration, becoming more challenging at a modest but steady rate of increase. As a result of this incremental approach, our bodies can adapt and absorb the benefits of these changes and respond by building strength and speed.

» Hill Repeats

A variation on Higher-Intensity Repeats is Hill Repeats. Instead of running on a track or other flat measured course for a specific distance (or time) at a higher-intensity level of effort and then jogging easily to recover in between, the athlete runs up a hill at a higher-intensity level of effort for the length of the repeat and then jogs back down the hill to the starting point between each Hill Repeat.

On the positive side, Hill Repeats build running power and prepare the athlete for more hilly marathon courses. On the flip side, these sessions can increase the risk of injury because the stress to the body is greater running up hills, and even more so running down hills. Only the programs in Chapter 5 designed for athletes who seldom are injured include Hill Repeats.

Chapter 5 includes suggestions on how to build Hill Repeats into any of the other programs as well. Please consider all of the variables before choosing to include Hill Repeats in your training plan. Your personal health and injury history should be considered, along with the specific topography of the marathon course you will be racing. If you do decide to include Hill Repeats in your marathon training program, be sure to utilize good running form to further minimize the risk of injury. In Chapter 10, "Secrets to Staying Injury-Free," we will present technique tips for running up and down hills.

Interestingly, many athletes think that the Higher-Intensity Repeat sessions are the most important of the TMBs. In typical "endurance athlete logic," these hurt the most so they must be the most beneficial. Here's some good news: Actually, the Higher-Intensity Repeat sessions are the least important of the three. In fact, certain athletes with specific injuries they are trying to work around may need to substitute a form of cross-training or possibly even skip Higher-Intensity Repeats entirely.

Higher-Intensity Repeats are undoubtedly the most stressful on the body of the Three Magic Bullets, so you should proceed with caution (see Chapter 10). The good news is that there are many over-forty athletes who very successfully cross-train their Higher-Intensity Repeats. In Chapters 3 and 5, we will introduce and discuss cross-training options for Higher-Intensity Repeats.

NOW FOR THE MAGIC PART!

After using our Three Magic Bullets training approach for years with many athletes, we have discovered that not only are these three workouts the key to achieving a marathon time goal, but they also can predict whether or not you can do it. You heard right! The Three Magic Bullets workouts can prepare you to achieve your goal time, *and* they can actually confirm to you before you step up to the starting line whether or not you are ready. In general, if you successfully follow one of our sixteen-week marathon training programs and run a smart race strategy on race day, your training results will roughly predict your race finishing time. We have found the following to be generally true for most athletes:

- If you can maintain your Target Marathon Pace in all of the Marathon Pacing Sessions up to and including the longest one of 80 minutes, and

- If you can run all of your Higher-Intensity Repeat sessions at 30 or more seconds per mile faster than your Target Marathon Pace, and

- If you can run all of your Long Runs at 30 to 60 seconds per mile slower than your Target Marathon Pace, then

- You are ready to run your goal time on race day—subject to proper pacing strategy, fueling and hydration, course, and weather conditions.

For example, if your goal is to maintain a Target Marathon Pace of 8:00 minutes per mile and break your previous best marathon time of 3:32, then:

- Your Marathon Pacing Sessions should be at a pace of 8:00 minutes per mile, and;

- Your Higher-Intensity Repeats should be at a pace of 7:30 minutes per mile or faster, and;

- Your Long Runs should be at a pace between 8:30 and 9:00 minutes per mile.

If you can achieve the paces for the respective sessions as shown in the example above, then you are ready to achieve your marathon goal on race day. This is wonderfully comforting to know prior to your race. It greatly reduces your pre-race stress and fear of the unknown. Instead of wondering if you can even do it, you know you can, and it just becomes a matter of executing properly on race day.

THE WEAKEST LINK

Here's another great benefit of the Three Magic Bullets sessions: They identify the areas requiring the greatest improvement early in your training program, giving you time to make adjustments and put greater focus on those areas before it is too late.

For example, what if you find that you can achieve your target paces on two of the three key workouts, but you cannot quite do it on the third? Say you can do the Higher-Intensity Repeats at 30 seconds or more faster than Target Marathon Pace, and you can do the Long Runs at 30 to 60 seconds slower than Target Marathon Pace, but you cannot quite hold target pace for the entire Marathon Pacing Session. What you have done is identify the weakest link in the equation. This is your area of weakness, where you need to put extra focus in your training.

Many athletes tend to avoid the workout they like the least. In fact, instead of focusing on their weak workout, we have seen many athletes skip it entirely and double up on one of the other workouts they prefer. Of course this is a flawed strategy. It's the ultimate in practicing what you are already good at and avoiding what you are not.

Some athletes do what we call "averaging them out." In other words, if they cannot meet the pacing target in one of the Three Magic Bullets sessions, they compensate by exceeding the pacing target in the other two. They rationalize that on average for the three sessions, they are actually ahead. But unfortunately it doesn't work that way. To know you are ready to achieve your marathon time, you need to be able to achieve the corresponding required times for each of the Three Magic Bullets.

When we discover weaknesses in our training, we should actually be excited. These are the keys to breaking through to another level of performance. By overcoming our weaknesses through the Three Magic Bullets sessions, we can take our performance to that higher level. As we like to say to our elite coached athletes, "Let's turn our weaknesses into strengths, and let's turn our strengths into weapons."

WHICH OF THE KEY WORKOUTS IS THE MOST IMPORTANT?

We are often asked which of the three key workouts is the most important. On an individual basis, the most important one for you is the one in which you have the greatest need for improvement.

Overall, however, for most athletes the Long Run is the most important. If you did no Higher-Intensity Repeats and no Marathon Pacing Sessions, but you did all of the Long Runs, you could still complete a marathon. You would not maximize your potential, but you would still be able to complete the distance on race day.

The least important workout for most marathoners is actually the Higher-Intensity Repeats. As mentioned earlier, many athletes feel that since these "hurt the most," they must therefore be the most beneficial. This is related to the old "no pain, no gain" adage that unfortunately many endurance athletes embrace. The reality for most marathoners is that this workout is the least important of the big three, which is significant because it is also often found to be the one most commonly associated with injury. Because of this, many of our fastest coached marathoners don't do Higher-Intensity Repeats in the form of running. We approach this component with proper cross-training options and other training methods. We will discuss this more in Chapters 3 and 5.

Now that you know about the Three Magic Bullets, we will move on to understanding how to properly build them into your overall training program, as well as how to effectively integrate our approach to cross-training in order to develop the optimal training program for the forty-plus marathoner.

But before we do, we present our first "40-Plus Athlete Success Story." At the end of each chapter, we will profile an athlete who achieved exceptional marathon results after turning forty and explain how he or she did it.

» PETER HYLAND:
40-Plus Athlete Success Story

Recently, forty-year-old Peter Hyland crossed the finish line in the New Jersey Marathon in a time of 2:49:41. Not only was his performance fast enough to place him in the top ten finishers overall, but it was also his fastest time ever and his first time under 2:50. Peter is living proof that it is possible to run your fastest marathons after turning forty.

Peter is married, has one child, and works as a chemist for a large pharmaceutical company. He has been a competitive runner for more than six years.

Amazingly, Peter's marathon training program typically includes only three runs per week—the Three Magic Bullets sessions discussed earlier in this chapter—plus two combination run/cross-training sessions. As a triathlete, Peter also swims and cycles a few times per week.

Peter's two weekly run/cross-training sessions embrace the "Free Running Miles" concept (see Chapter 3). They are both "Transition Sessions," which begin with a longer bike ride and end with a short run. Overall, Peter's training averages only five hours per week of actual running for the entire year, and peaks at only about seven hours of actual running in his biggest training weeks leading up to his marathons.

Peter's least favorite workout of the Three Magic Bullets is the Marathon Pacing Session, but he credits this challenging workout as one of the keys to continually lowering his marathon times.

With efficient and well-structured training, and by embracing the concept of "free miles," Peter has been able to maximize his results while minimizing injuries. With his winning approach, Peter Hyland will definitely be running many more fast marathons after forty!

» *The Recovery Trick*

Don't be afraid to give up the good to go for the great. —STEVE PREFONTAINE

The biggest difference between athletes under forty and those over forty is in the time required for recovery. As we get older, the time period needed to fully absorb the benefits of a particular workout and to be prepared for the next workout gradually lengthens. As the human body ages, its ability to repair itself and regenerate slows down. Our joints become stiffer and our range of motion decreases. The human body also becomes less resilient to impact, and of course running, especially on harder surfaces, creates a great deal of impact.

Not only do older athletes need to train in new ways, but as you will see later in this book, they need to battle these natural changes in their bodies by becoming more resilient through proper core and strength training, dynamic warm-up, stretching, nutrition, and a more proactive approach to their health.

The changes that come with aging are also part of the reason older athletes are more prone to injury. Many attempt the same training volume they did when they were younger. Typically they try to do the same number of workouts, at the same intensity level and duration as they did at a younger

Aya Stevens, elite runner and professional triathlete
James Mitchell Photography

age, and the result can often be frustrating. Many athletes don't fully understand what is meant by training volume. They often confuse volume and duration, equating volume with how many miles run. But miles run is only part of what is meant by training volume. Training volume is the combination of how long you run, how intense your effort level is while you run, and how frequently you run. Training volume is best expressed by the following equation:

$$\textit{Training Volume = Duration x Intensity x Frequency}$$

Not only do the workouts themselves need to change in terms of duration and intensity as we get older, but the frequency at which we do them also needs to change.

ACTIVE RECOVERY DAYS

One approach might be simply to run three days per week instead of six days per week like we used to do when we were younger. Perhaps just do the TMB sessions every other day and nothing else. Running every other day, instead of every day, would allow us forty-eight hours of complete rest between workouts instead of the twenty-four hours we used to allow.

On the plus side, we would likely find that we would not get injured as often with this type of every-other-day approach. The problem with this training strategy, however, is that we would probably discover that we are training far less than needed to remain as competitive as we would like. This is very frustrating for the maturing athlete.

It is important to understand that there are two ways to recover between challenging workouts. We can recover through complete rest, and we can also recover actively with some type of running or other physical activity. There is a place for both complete rest days and active recovery days in every athlete's training program. Sometimes complete rest is the best option, while in other situations some type of active recovery is more beneficial. The optimal training strategy for most marathoners is to run six days a week with one complete rest day. The six running days would include the TMB sessions spaced every other day, with moderate aerobic run days positioned between the TMB days. The moderate aerobic runs are an example of the active recovery that we often suggest for many of our younger coached athletes, as well as for many of our forty-plus coached athletes who rarely become injured. We will present marathon training programs with this type of structure in Chapter 5.

But even moderate aerobic run days between the TMB days may be too much running for some, if not most, forty-plus athletes. This number of running days and overall running volume will not allow many forty-plus athletes to recover, build stronger and faster, and stay healthy. Or in other words, the combined run duration, intensity, and frequency is too much for the athlete to absorb and benefit from.

The secret for these athletes is this: Instead of doing a moderate aerobic run on the days between key workout sessions, substitute a moderate non-running aerobic training session. Not only do moderate non-running sessions allow for a forty-eight-hour recovery period between TMB sessions, but they also continue to build fitness and endurance on the recovery day.

Just think about how beneficial that can be for a marathoner. We can actively recover on the days in between while continuing to train and build toward our marathon goal. We not only receive great training benefit on the recovery days, but we also become refreshed and ready to put out a great effort in our next Magic Bullets session on the following day.

So, for most forty-plus athletes, the optimal marathon training approach is going to be either the TMB sessions with two to three moderate aerobic run days in between, or the TMB sessions with two or three moderate cross-training sessions in between. The sixteen-week training programs included in Chapter 5 will present options for both of these scenarios.

Why is it so important to have sufficient recovery time, either in the form of a rest day or an active recovery day, after each of the Magic Bullet sessions?

You can make an analogy comparing any of our key workouts to a medical operation. Each of the TMBs does something to the body to help it to improve, but only after the body has time to rest, recover, and absorb the benefits of the workout will it actually achieve the value of the training session. If someone has a medical operation and then immediately jumps up and runs out of the operating room, we would guess that in most cases the planned benefits of the operation will not be achieved, and perhaps the patient will be even worse off than before the procedure. Likewise, after one of the TMB workouts, we require sufficient rest, recovery, nutrition, and time for the workout to have its effects. If we complete one of the TMB sessions and then do not sleep or eat for forty-eight hours, or do some other equally challenging physical activity, the benefit of the workout will not be achieved. In fact, the athlete will more likely end up weaker, slower, and possibly injured or ill.

In a recent *Runner's World* article titled "Ryan's Hope," writer Amby Burfoot quotes Ryan Hall, a top American marathoner: "For a long time, I lacked confidence to back off on easy days. As a result, my body couldn't absorb all of the great training. Now I have the confidence to run easy on recovery days, so I can bring the fire for hard workouts and race days." Hall adds, "When you're sleeping, your body absorbs all the hard work. It's ironic: One of the best ways to get better is to do nothing."

Many athletes don't understand this concept. To properly train your body, you need to allow time for recovery or the training session doesn't work. Another way to look at this is that the workout is not really over until the required recovery period has been completed.

How much rest and recovery is required? This is the tricky part, and the place where most athletes go wrong. The real answer is that it varies from athlete to athlete. But it is definitely the case that additional rest and recovery are required as we get older. In general, however, we find that most over-forty athletes need to space each of their TMBs out by two days. In other words, doing any of them on back-to-back days increases the risk of injury.

A common way to space out the TMBs within an athlete's training week would be to do the Higher-Intensity Repeats on Tuesday, the Marathon Pacing Session on Thursday, and the Long Run on Saturday.

So what do you do on the days in between? This is where the "trick" comes in. We want to maximize the benefits of those recovery days between the TMBs. Depending on your age, health, injury history, experience, and other factors, what you do on those days in between may range from a run, to some type of cross-training activity, to a complete rest day.

In Chapter 5, we will present several specific training plan options that fit each of these scenarios. Based on your specific situation, you will be able to select the one that fits you the best.

Let's look at a perfect setup. If we were coaching a very experienced forty plus runner who rarely had an injury, we would most likely suggest a plan involving each of the TMB workouts, spaced two days apart. Then on the days in between, we would suggest a moderate aerobic run, in the range of 65–85 percent of maximum heart rate (Heart Rate Zone Z1 to Z2). Finally, we would suggest one complete rest day each week.

One possible version of this plan would be the following:

- Monday: Moderate Aerobic Run #1

- Tuesday: Higher-Intensity Repeats

- Wednesday: Moderate Aerobic Run #2

- Thursday: Marathon Pacing Session

- Friday: Moderate Aerobic Run #3

- Saturday: Long Run

- Sunday: Rest Day

There is a definite advantage to this approach. Each of the TMBs puts a great amount of physical stress on the body and requires about two days for most over-forty athletes to adequately recover and absorb the benefits. While we could do this by taking a complete rest day, we can achieve the same thing with a moderate run. The moderate run still allows the athlete to recover from the TMB session the previous day and provides him with additional aerobic conditioning. Not only does it allow the runner to recover, but at the same time it also builds his fitness.

This is a very powerful combination and lies at the heart of a successful marathon program. So many athletes get this part of their training wrong. We will expand on common training mistakes to be avoided in Chapter 12. But we will mention here two of the big ones that frequently occur. First, some athletes will group two or more of the TMBs too closely together, not allowing for sufficient recovery. The other common mistake is to go too hard on the moderate aerobic run day. This relates to both the flawed "no pain, no gain" and "more is always better" philosophies mentioned in Chapter 1. The "no pain, no gain" athlete incorrectly believes that if the moderate aerobic run feels comfortable, it cannot possibly be doing any good. He believes he needs to be suffering or he is wasting his time. The "more is always better" athlete thinks that if these runs are useful at a moderate pace, then they must be even better at a fast pace. This is also incorrect.

In fact, not only does the moderate aerobic run fail to help if it is done harder or faster, but it also may actually negate the training benefit from the athlete's TMB workout the day before. And if you go too hard on the moderate aerobic days, you will not be rested enough to maximize the training benefit from the TMB session the following day. You then start to fall into a common "junk training" cycle: Your "hard" days are not hard enough and your "easy" days are not easy enough. Everything sort of ends up in the middle range, and the purpose of each individual workout in your weekly training cycle is lost.

COMPLETE REST DAYS

Typically we suggest at least one complete rest day per week. Optimally, the forty-plus athlete would do the Three Magic Bullets workouts with the three moderate aerobic sessions on the days in between. It is important to get these six workouts right and then allow your body an entire day to recover and absorb all the good training benefits. This will reduce the risk of injury and keep the athlete fresher and more mentally motivated.

Our experience working with athletes for several decades has demonstrated that weekly rest days are a big part of the "recovery trick." Athletes who consistently plan for these rest days are typically healthier, have fewer interruptions to their training, and are more likely to achieve their long-term goals. Most importantly, they tend to enjoy the journey much more. On the other hand, athletes who do not include a complete rest day once a week tend to be injured more often and become frustrated because they usually do not achieve their potential. Many just get mentally burned out on running for a while.

One possible exception to the weekly rest day for certain athletes may be swimming. Some of our coached triathletes have an optional swim day on their rest day. Since swimming involves physical movement with little or no impact, it can actually serve as an excellent active recovery for some runners. This of course assumes that the athlete is getting proper sleep and nutrition, but many athletes report feeling even more recovered from a swim day than a complete rest day.

We have seen many athletes over the years get extremely involved with their marathon preparation and really go overboard in their training. They let the delicate balance between enough and too much get out of sync. These athletes may make it to the starting line, but they are mentally and physically worn out by this point, and their performance is disappointing. Then, after their marathon, they end up "crashing" for a few months. They feel the need to get away from training for a while, so they take a couple of months off, gain weight, and get the "post-marathon blues." Eventually they return to their training, but find that it takes a long time just to get back to a good level of fitness, let alone great marathon form. They then end up doing some type of "crash-course training" to catch up on lost time and quickly get ready for another marathon. Again, reality does not meet expectations. They typically find that they do not improve much over their last marathon and may even race more slowly this time.

This is especially true for the over-forty athlete who is likely to decondition faster and take even longer than his younger counterpart to return to his prior fitness level. There is an old saying that it takes twice as long to get back into shape as it does to get out of shape in the first place. We have generally found this to be true for all athletes, and possibly even more so for most forty-plus athletes.

Many athletes follow this type of cycle year after year. They overtrain ten months of the year and then do nothing athletically for two months. Their performances never seem to improve much, so they eventually conclude that they have reached their potential. More likely, they haven't yet come close to achieving their potential.

The opposite of this is the runner who takes a rest day every week, plus a few extra ones here and there over the year when they need them—perhaps for holidays or travel days, or other occasional situations. These athletes are able to train year-round, stay healthier, and remain mentally motivated. Not surprisingly, these athletes also improve more. Year after year they keep lowering their personal best times, even after reaching forty.

Here's the really amazing surprise in the above comparison. On an annual basis, both types of athletes train approximately the same number of days and have the same number of rest days. The smart athlete ends up with about sixty rest days per year (one per week, plus a few others now and then when needed), and the not-so-smart athlete ends up with about sixty rest days (consecutively over a two-month period). When you look at it this way, it's easy to see why one athlete has so much more success than the other.

What if running six days a week is too much running? For many athletes, running six days a week is too much. Because of their age, prior injury conditions, or even their biomechanics, they cannot avoid injury when running six days a week. We have worked with many such athletes over the years. Cross-training is the answer for over-forty athletes. The three weekly moderate aerobic runs can be replaced successfully with appropriate moderate cross-training activities.

But can you do a marathon on only three days a week of actual running? The answer is yes. Bottom line, if we do the TMB workouts each week, and for reasons of time management or health history cannot add any additional run sessions, a successful marathon is still possible. In fact, one of the marathon training programs in Chapter 5 has only one and a half actual run sessions; cross-training is substituted for the Higher-Intensity Repeats and half of the Long Run. Only the Marathon Pacing Session is 100 percent running.

The most common scenario is not that the athlete cannot do more than the TMB workouts for time management reasons, but because of the risk of injury. So, if your body is telling you that you can no longer even run three times a week and stay healthy, don't be discouraged. With proper cross-training, you can still prepare for marathons with as few as one and a half actual runs per week, and you can be competitive on as little as three actual runs per week. There is a marathon training program for you.

What are some cross-training options and how can you select the best one? Chapter 3 will present the most successful cross-training activities for marathon training and not only explain the pros and cons of each, but also describe exactly how they compare with one another in terms of marathon training benefits.

» KELLIE BROWN:
40-Plus Athlete Success Story

Kellie Brown is married and a practicing veterinarian. She has been a competitive runner and triathlete for more than twelve years and has completed more than twenty-five marathons.

Kellie successfully qualified for the Boston Marathon several times prior to turning forty and had a personal best of 3:37. After turning forty, however, she continued to improve her times and has been achieving the Boston qualifying standard by increasingly greater margins.

Kellie credits her ability to run faster marathons after forty to continually learning to train smarter and more efficiently. Effective cross-training has been a key element in this. In fact, Kellie feels that her marathoning became significantly better when she started cross-training and preparing for triathlons.

Kellie also now uses heart-rate training in her program, and we build her marathon training plans around the Three Magic Bullets workouts. Kellie's favorite of the three is the Marathon Pacing Session, as she enjoys its great challenge.

At the time of this writing, Kellie's personal best times were steadily improving, and she was already down into the 3:20s. A sub-3:20 performance seems likely for the future. Most importantly, however, Kellie enjoys the entire marathoning journey. She has made many lifelong friends through the sport, and she loves to inspire others and use her running success to support good causes.

Kellie Brown will be running many more fast marathons after forty!

» Free Running Miles

We run, not because we think it is doing us good, but because we enjoy it and cannot help ourselves. . . . The more restricted our society and work become, the more necessary it will be to find some outlet for this craving for freedom. No one can say, "You must not run faster than this, or jump higher than that." The human spirit is indomitable.

—SIR ROGER BANNISTER

Running six days a week is often not the best approach for the forty-plus athlete. As discussed in the previous chapter on recovery, some athletes can get away with this due to their unique biomechanics

Nuta Olaru, Masters Marathon champion

101 Degrees West

and clear injury history, but most over-forty athletes find that this amount of running leads to injury and frustration.

The optimal training program for that special athlete who rarely gets injured would likely include the TMB sessions each week, spaced out every other day, with moderate aerobic runs on the three days in between, plus a rest day to complete the weekly training cycle. But it's important to note that the six runs per week approach is not necessary to run fast marathons. There are other options for the many forty-plus athletes who find that this volume of running leads to injury. Exciting cross-training approaches are available that have the same or almost the same training benefit as the six runs per week approach, but with far less risk of injury.

This chapter includes our specific approaches to cross-training that allow the athlete to make smart running substitutions, resulting in "Free Running Miles," which minimize the physical stress on the legs and body associated with hard road surfaces. By Free Running Miles, we are referring to activities that provide a training benefit similar to actual running, but do not carry some of the negatives of running (e.g., high impact).

We often joke with athletes prone to running-related injuries that what we want to do is get as close as we can to preparing for a marathon without actually running. While it seems impossible to be able to prepare for a marathon without running, as you will see in this chapter, we can come surprisingly close to that goal.

Let us remind you first to check out any aches, pains, or other health concerns with your doctor before you attempt any of the training approaches presented in this book. Always fully explain any training plan you intend to use to your doctor in advance and get his or her approval before you begin.

We will start by introducing several approaches to cross-training and then conclude this chapter with a presentation of the "Free Miles Training Hierarchy." Determining your level in the Free Miles Training Hierarchy will be a major consideration in selecting the optimal marathon training program for you.

CROSS-TRAINING TRANSITION SESSIONS

One of the most effective techniques to get Free Running Miles is through Transition Sessions. These types of sessions are popular with triathletes, and they are commonly referred to as "Bricks."

An example of a typical Transition Session is to cycle for 45 minutes and then immediately change into running gear and go for a 15-minute run. This is a good example of what we are referring to as Free Running Miles. While this 60-minute workout is not a 60-minute run, the cardio training benefits are equal, or at least very close to equal, to a 60-minute run. The great advantage of this type of Transition Session is that while the aerobic benefits are present for the entire 60 minutes, the negative impact of pounding away on the roads is greatly reduced.

At the end of Chapter 1, we profiled an athlete we coach named Peter Hyland, an over-forty marathoner who records times in the 2:40s. Peter uses this Free Running Miles technique most of the time. Typically he does only three "pure runs" per week when training for a marathon—the Three Magic Bullets. His other two weekly runs are actually Transition Sessions. He starts with a longer bike ride, then quickly changes from his bike gear to his running gear and goes for a shorter run. As a triathlete, Peter of course cycles and swims, but amazingly his time spent running each week averages only about five hours over the course of the year. This increases to a weekly average more like seven hours when he is in peak training for a marathon, but his allotted running time is relatively low compared to most marathoners, let alone elite age-group marathoners.

As mentioned in Peter Hyland's profile, not only did he get faster after he turned forty, but he even lowered his times into the 2:40s for the first time. Many athletes would not believe such a fast time possible with so little running. But Peter and his excellent approach to cross-training proves that it is possible. What's more, Peter doesn't have a running background. He did not race in high school or college and didn't start competitive road racing until he was in his mid-thirties.

There are many ways an athlete can build Transition Sessions into his weekly training program to get Free Running Miles. The following is one example:

- Monday: Rest Day

- Tuesday: Higher-Intensity Run Repeats

- Wednesday: Transition Session—bike ride followed by moderate short run

- Thursday: Marathon Pacing Session

- Friday: Transition Session—bike ride followed by moderate short run

- Saturday: Long Run

- Sunday: Bike ride

This is just one possible example for using Transition Sessions for Free Running Miles. Chapter 5 will offer additional guidance on how to effectively build this concept into specific marathon training programs.

The above example utilizes cycling as the cross-training activity. But there are many possible cross-training activities, and we will discuss the pros and cons of each later in this chapter. Cycling often works best for triathletes, because it is an activity they are already doing. It's just a matter of building it into their training program in a way that serves both their marathon and triathlon goals. But cycling may or may not be the best cross-training activity for you.

One additional tip on Transition Sessions: These are great workouts to do inside. If weather conditions or darkness make outside training difficult, Transition Sessions can easily be done indoors with a treadmill and another type of cross-training equipment, like a stationary bike or elliptical trainer.

If you want to really add to the challenge and make the time pass quickly, try double or even triple Transition Sessions. Instead of just a single transition from cycling to running, these sessions involve multiple transitions, back and forth, between cycling and running.

Following is an example of a 60-minute Double Transition Session:

15-minute run (quick change)—30-minute bike (quick change)—
15-minute run

Following is an example of a 60-minute Triple Transition Session:

15-minute run (quick change)—15-minute bike (quick change)—
15-minute run (quick change)—15-minute bike

Another challenging option with multiple Transition Sessions is to include more than one cross-training option. The following is an example of a 60-minute Triple Transition Session utilizing both the stationary bike and the elliptical trainer:

15-minute run (quick change)—15-minute bike (quick change)—
15-minute run (quick change)—15-minute elliptical trainer

These are all fun and challenging 60-minute moderate aerobic sessions. They provide Free Running Miles and are especially helpful for making those indoor training sessions fly by.

Transition sessions are just one option and are not optimal for all runners. For many athletes the TMB workouts involve all the running they can handle without risk of injury. For them, straight cross-training sessions substituted for the two to three weekly moderate aerobic sessions typically work best.

It's hard for many athletes to believe that doing only three (or even fewer) runs per week combined with cross-training is enough. But if it's done correctly, it most definitely is enough. Not only are many successful forty-plus athletes racing fast marathons doing only three runs a week, but they also are greatly increasing their chances of being able to continue racing and training for many years to come. If built properly into an athlete's program, cross-training puts far less physical stress on the athlete's body. So while she can still achieve the desired training benefits, she is able to do it without the wear and tear from running six days a week on hard road surfaces.

There are many ways an athlete can build these cross-training sessions into a weekly training program to get Free Running Miles. The following is one example:

- Monday: Rest Day

- Tuesday: Higher-Intensity Run Repeats

- Wednesday: Moderate Aerobic Bike Ride #1

- Thursday: Marathon Pacing Session

- Friday: Moderate Aerobic Bike Ride #2

- Saturday: Long Run

- Sunday: Moderate Aerobic Bike Ride #3

Additional examples will be presented in the sixteen-week marathon training programs in Chapter 5. Again, the above example utilizes cycling as the cross-training activity, but there are many possible cross-training activities to choose from.

CROSS-TRAINING OPTIONS

Following are what we find to be the most popular and beneficial cross-training methods, presented in the order of how closely they simulate actual running.

- Treadmill running

- Deep-water running

- Cross-country skiing

- Elliptical training

- Cycling

- Hill walking

- Swimming

Now that you understand the possibilities of using both Transition Sessions and straight cross-training sessions in your marathon training, we will discuss each of the possible cross-training activities and their pros and cons, to help you select the best activity for your situation and learn how to build it into your specific training program.

Specificity is the key. The closer the cross-training option mirrors actual running the better. By this we mean that the actual combination of muscle movements between running and the cross-training option are fairly similar.

One cross-training option is nearly identical to actual running. Treadmill running is so similar to road running that most runners consider it to be the same thing. Stationary cycling, on the other hand, uses many of the same muscle groups, but the motion is clearly different. In most cases the treadmill is a better running substitution than the stationary bike.

Now here's the tricky part: If you have an injury that is aggravated by running, the closer the cross-training activity is to actual running, the greater the chance that the cross-training activity will also aggravate the injury. So what is the perfect cross-training substitution for an athlete with a specific running injury? All else being equal, it's the one that gets the closest to mimicking actual running without aggravating the injury. If you have an injury, you should always get your doctor's approval in advance of any activity, but the list above can help you to select the best cross-training activity, given your specific injury.

Stated simply, the highest activity on the list that does not aggravate your condition is the one probably best suited for you. But as you will see, access and convenience to these activities is another big consideration when selecting the best cross-training activity. For example, deep-water running may not aggravate your injury, but if you do not have convenient access to a pool, then it is not a good running substitute. Convenience and availability are also important considerations when selecting your cross-training options.

» Treadmill Running

The treadmill is the most popular cross-training activity for running because it is so closely related to actual outside running. In fact, most athletes don't even consider it cross-training. Yet this is not 100 percent the case because the treadmill does cause us to slightly modify our running biomechanics. Our body actually uses a somewhat different motion to run over a stable surface than it does to run in place over a moving surface. But running on the treadmill is almost exactly the same as outside running.

Advantages of Treadmill Training

- The biomechanics are the closest to outside running of any of the cross-training options.

- It offers a softer and more even surface that greatly reduces the physical stress on the runner's body compared to running on the roads.

- It allows the athlete to train even when weather conditions or darkness prevents outside running.

- It helps to practice pacing for workouts like the Marathon Pacing Session.

- It's easy to practice your fueling and hydration plan; you can set up your fueling and hydration sources on or next to the treadmill.

- You can do multiple things at once: Not only can you watch television or listen to music while you run, we even know athletes who find that they spend more time with their families. Instead of disappearing out the door for an hour, they can remain at home while running.

- Safety: Typically treadmill training is done in the safety and security of your home or at a fitness center.

Disadvantages of Treadmill Training

- Many athletes find indoor treadmill running to be boring. Some jokingly call the treadmill the "dread mill." Some find that they can reduce or eliminate this disadvantage by watching television, movies, or listening to music. But many athletes struggle with this issue.

- Treadmill running is not outdoors. Many athletes say getting outside and enjoying nature is their favorite part of running.

- Treadmill running is so close to outside running that if an athlete has a particular injury for which he is using cross-training for recovery, treadmill running may aggravate the injury as much as outdoor running. So listen to your body and only use this cross-training option if you can do so pain-free.

Additional Treadmill Tips

The treadmill can be so helpful for reducing the wear and tear of running on hard roads that we often suggest that forty-plus runners work some treadmill running into their overall program—not just when they are injured, but year-round.

How much is the right amount? We suggest starting out by substituting it for one run per week—even for one of the Three Magic Bullets sessions—and see how it feels. We know of many athletes who alternate all their runs between the treadmill and outdoors. In other words, if you do one run outside, try your next run on the treadmill, and continue this sequence. This is a great approach for many runners and maximizes the benefits of both outdoor and treadmill running.

Many athletes believe that treadmill running is easier than actual running because there is no wind resistance. Accordingly, many athletes compensate by setting the grade at a 1 percent incline. This is worth considering; however, check with your treadmill vendor to make sure this is appropriate with your specific treadmill model.

Although not readily available yet, there are many other new innovative treadmill options including aquatic, zero-gravity, and split-track treadmills.

>> Deep-Water Running

Deep-water pool running is a great cross-training option because it has virtually no impact and can be helpful with a wide range of running injuries.

What we mean by deep-water running is to use a flotation belt to keep you afloat in deep water and then to run in place, mimicking your running form as closely as possible. Your feet do not come in contact with the bottom of the pool. The water actually creates natural resistance, which adds to the benefit of the workout. You can also wear resistance footwear, which increases your cardiovascular workout and strengthens your lower body.

Flotation belts and resistance footwear can be purchased at most swim shops and are often available at a pool that has water aerobic classes.

Advantages of Deep-Water Running

- It has virtually no impact, which allows you to get most of the positive conditioning benefits of running without the impact to joints and soft tissue.

- The natural resistance provided by the water builds strength and endurance.

Disadvantages of Deep-Water Running

- Most athletes find it to be boring. Staring at the wall next to the indoor pool is nowhere near as enjoyable as running outside on a beautiful trail through the woods. Many athletes partially negate this by listening to music while they pool run or turn and face a different direction periodically, staring at four different walls instead of just one.

- The density of the water does not allow you to perfectly mimic your actual run form. It's fairly close but not exactly the same as actual running.

- It can be inconvenient; unless you have your own pool, or at least a pool located close to your home or place of work, significant travel time may be involved, or pool availability may not fit in with your schedule.

- Safety: You should not attempt deep-water running unless you are a competent swimmer. You also should only deep-water run in a safe body of water with a competent lifeguard on duty.

» Cross-Country Skiing or Cross-Country Ski Machine

This is one of the most effective cross-training substitutions for running. Not surprisingly, many elite cross-country skiers are also fast runners. While actual outdoor cross-country skiing is only available in certain climates and at limited times of the year, cross-country ski machines bring this exercise to anyone, just about anywhere.

Once while training for an Iron-Distance triathlon, Don had an injury that would not allow him to actually run, so he did virtually all of his run training over a three-month period on a cross-country ski machine. He was amazed at how close his marathon time split in that particular Iron-Distance triathlon compared to other Iron-Distance marathons he had run prior to it. It was within 2 percent of his best times.

Advantages of Cross-Country Skiing or the Cross-Country Ski Machine

- It utilizes many of the same muscle groups as actual running and is an especially good substitute for running.

- It is relatively low impact.

- It also helps to build core and upper-body strength.

- A cross-country ski machine is a relatively inexpensive piece of equipment compared to a treadmill.

- Like a treadmill, a cross-country ski machine in your home allows you to do many things at once (e.g., watch television, watch movies, listen to music, spend time with your family, etc.).

Disadvantages of Cross-Country Skiing or the Cross-Country Ski Machine

- Actual outdoor skiing is only available in certain climate zones and even then, only at certain times of the year.

- Cross-country ski machines are not as popular as other endurance exercise equipment, like treadmills and elliptical machines, so there is less chance you will have one available to you at a fitness center.

- There is some level of experience required. If you do not know how to cross-country ski, it can be ineffective at best, and downright dangerous at worst. You should only attempt this if you have a good instructor to show you proper technique and help you to get started.

» Elliptical Training

This is also a great cross-training option and probably the one that we personally use the most. We have one set up in our workout room and enjoy using it while either watching television or listening to music.

Advantages of Elliptical Training

- It's convenient; most fitness centers offer a wide variety of elliptical machines, or you can purchase one for your own home.

- While not a perfect running movement, it does use many of the same muscle groups as actual running.

- It's relatively low impact, so it greatly reduces the impact on joints and soft tissue.

- Like a treadmill, an elliptical machine in your home allows you to do many things at once (e.g., watch television, watch movies, listen to music, spend time with your family, etc.).

- There are many different types of elliptical machines, each with its own unique motion. You can select the one that feels best to you.

Disadvantages of Elliptical Training

- It is not a perfect substitution for running. While better than most, we would rank it behind treadmill running, pool running, and a cross-country ski machine in terms of how well it simulates your running form and uses the same muscle groups.

» *Outdoor Cycling and Indoor Stationary Bike*

Actual outdoor cycling or indoor cycling on a stationary bike is one of the most popular means of cross-training. It's an activity just about everyone has experience with, and if you don't have a bike or stationary bike at home, stationary bikes are readily available at most fitness centers.

It's probably the most popular cross-training option with triathletes training for a marathon, because it's an activity they already include as part of their routine. If they need to cut down on their running miles due to an injury or some other issue, it's easy for them to balance it out by increasing the cycling component of their overall training plan. They also get a "two-for-one" benefit with cycling. It helps their training for triathlons, and it also provides Free Running Miles.

Peter Hyland, the athlete profiled in Chapter 1, is a good example of this type of athlete. His actual running volume is relatively low thanks to all of the cycling he does to prepare for triathlons. As pointed out, he averages only about five hours of running per week year-round, and only about seven hours per week during specific marathon training phases. This is relatively light for an athlete who runs marathons in the 2:40s.

Advantages of Outdoor Cycling and Indoor Stationary Bike

- It's convenient and easy to go for a bike ride or use a stationary bike at home or at a fitness center.

- It's relatively low impact.

- It's triathlon compatible: Cycling is often the best means of cross-training for a triathlete because they are already training in this sport. If they need a running substitution due to injury, they can increase the cycling portion of their training and decrease the running portion.

Disadvantages of Outdoor Cycling and Indoor Stationary Bike

- It uses many of the same muscle groups as running, but cycling is a different movement, and we rate it as less effective than some of the other options.

- Safety: Outdoor cycling can be dangerous. Falls and crashes are common with this activity.

>> *Hill Walking*

Only fairly recently have we experimented with hill walking as a possible running substitution, and we have been pleasantly surprised with what we have experienced. The best way to hill walk is on a treadmill, where you can set the grade at a constant elevation and simulate walking up a long hill. This activity engages many of the same muscle groups as running, especially the glutes, it's lower impact than running, and at a challenging grade (most treadmills allow you to increase the grade up to 10 or 15 percent), you can get your heart rate into the aerobic zone.

Obviously it is a better substitute to run on the treadmill if possible, but you may find that an injury aggravated by running on the treadmill feels much better while hill walking on the treadmill.

>> *Swimming*

Even though we are both swimmers, we don't rate swimming as a particularly good cross-training option for running. It focuses mainly on different muscle groups, and the motion of kicking does not mimic actual running. Swimming is a good substitute because it is a good form of aerobic exercise and a relatively low-impact form of exercise, but nothing beyond that pertains to running.

Swimming is also a technique sport. This means that unless you already have good swimming technique, it becomes even less of a good running substitute. Furthermore, poor swimming form can cause injury.

We would only suggest swimming as a running substitute for those athletes who already have good swimming form and do not have any better cross-training options available or, because of the nature of their injury, find it is the only cross-training option available to them.

If you do decide to swim, only do so in a safe body of water and under the supervision of a competent lifeguard.

SUBSTITUTIONS FOR THE THREE MAGIC BULLETS

So far we have talked about cross-training substitutions for purposes of helping with injury recovery and also for replacing the three weekly moderate aerobic sessions in our standard six runs per week marathon training plan. We know that cross-training has value when weather conditions or darkness make running tough. Another purpose for cross-training can include Three Magic Bullets substitutions.

If possible, our first preference would be to substitute cross-training options for the moderate aerobic sessions, but due to either injury or inclement weather conditions, it is also possible to substitute cross-training options for at least two of the Three Magic Bullets sessions.

The treadmill easily works as a substitute for all three of them. In fact, many athletes frequently prefer to use the treadmill for any or all of the TMBs. To a limited extent, other cross-training options can be used for TMB substitutions:

- **Higher-Intensity Repeat Sessions:** The treadmill works great for these sessions because it allows you to easily control your pace, which fits this type of training session very well. You simply dial up the speed for the Higher-Intensity Repeat portions and then decrease it for the recovery interval in between, as well as for the warm-up and cooldown. Most of the other cross-training options work for Higher-Intensity Repeats too, because the effort level for the high-intensity part and the recovery intervals is the key aspect of the workout. Pacing is secondary.

- **Marathon Pacing Sessions:** The treadmill also works well with this workout because it allows you to dial in your exact target pace for the entire pacing portion. Unfortunately, however, none of the other cross-training options work particularly well as substitutes for this session, as pacing is the key aspect of this workout.

- **Long Runs:** Long Runs on the treadmill can be boring but effective. The treadmill reduces impact and may keep your legs fresher. Most of the other cross-training options work fairly well as a substitute for the Long Run session, but only on a temporary basis. Again, effort level is more important than pacing for this particular training session. If an athlete needs to use a cross-training option to work through a relatively short-term injury, cross-training will work as a Long Run substitution. But ultimately a majority of the Long Runs should include some outdoor running.

So the treadmill works very well for each of the big three. As we move down the hierarchy of cross-training options, however, the ability to use other means of cross-training becomes less and less effective. This is particularly true for the workouts involving specific pace work. If you do use other cross-training options for the TMB sessions, you should try to estimate how the desired pace feels on a perceived effort basis and then do your best to simulate it.

One of the best approaches to running fast marathons after forty is to take advantage of Free Running Miles and sensibly build them into your training program. In general, however, for those athletes who find it difficult to stay 100 percent healthy doing the optimal six runs per week (the TMBs, separated by three moderate aerobic sessions), our suggestion is to first consider running your Three Magic Bullets and cross-training your three moderate aerobic sessions. If that is still too much running, the next step is to consider substituting cross-training for some of your TMB sessions.

As you will see in Chapter 5, we have one training plan option that utilizes running for the Marathon Pacing Session, running for half of the Long Run, which is structured as a Transition Session, and then cross-training options for the Higher-Intensity Repeat session and all the moderate aerobic sessions. In other words, it's marathon training doing as few as one and a half actual runs per week. If even a small amount of running tends to cause injury issues for you, this type of approach may be something you want to consider in consultation with your doctor.

FREE MILES TRAINING HIERARCHY

Now that we have discussed the concept of Transition Sessions, reviewed the best cross-training options, and discussed how best to substitute them for the moderate aerobic runs and the TMB sessions, we will introduce what we like to refer to as the "Free Miles Training Hierarchy." You need to look at your unique situation and history and determine where you stand on the scale of being able to do virtually all your training in the form of running, or being able to do only a very small amount of training in the form of running. This scale is the Free Miles Training Hierarchy:

- **Level 1:** The TMB sessions and the two to three moderate aerobic sessions per week are all completed in the form of actual running.

- **Level 2:** The TMB sessions are completed in the form of actual running, and the two to three moderate aerobic sessions are completed in the form of Transition Sessions.

- **Level 3:** The TMB sessions are completed in the form of actual running, and the two to three moderate aerobic sessions are completed in the form of cross-training.

- **Level 4:** Of the three TMB sessions, one or more is completed in the form of actual running, while the others are completed in the form of Transition Sessions and/or cross-training; the two to three moderate aerobic sessions are completed in the form of cross-training.

By honestly assessing your individual situation, you can determine where you fall on the Free Miles Training Hierarchy. By doing so, you will be well positioned to select the optimal type of marathon training program for you. In Chapter 5, we will present various sixteen-week marathon training programs to fit all four levels of the Free Miles Training Hierarchy, and include tips on how to adjust these plans to fit your specific needs.

» CARL CURRAN:
40-Plus Athlete Success Story

Carl Curran's marathon journey started on a day of tragedy. As an investment banker working in lower Manhattan, he experienced the horror of September 11, 2001, on the front line. This life-changing experience had a deep impact and caused him to take his wife and children on a sabbatical. This time of contemplation led to a new lifestyle, including a renewed focus on good health.

Carl changed his life. He lost more than fifty pounds over the next year and entered his first marathon in 2002 at the age of thirty-seven. He recorded a time of 3:28 at the New York City Marathon that year and has since completed more than ten additional marathons. In his first ten marathons he successfully qualified for the Boston Marathon an impressive eight times.

Carl improved from his first marathon, consistently lowering his times at each subsequent marathon through smart and efficient training. Due to a low injury occurrence to date, Carl has been able to maintain a relatively high-volume running program. As with many athletes we coach, Carl enjoys his long training runs the most and his Marathon Pacing Sessions the least, but credits this particular Magic Bullet session as one of the keys to his steady improvement.

In April 2009, Carl set a new personal best of 3:05 at the Boston Marathon. The day after Boston, Don e-mailed Carl both to congratulate him on his great success and also to let him know that he wanted him to create a little sign that simply read "2:57 Chicago" and post it on his bathroom mirror. Don said this would be the first thing he would see every day for the next twenty-four weeks, and it would serve as a powerful motivator in preparation for the Chicago Marathon in October.

Twenty-four weeks later at the Chicago Marathon, Carl crossed the finish line in 2:57. Not only was this his first sub-3-hour performance, but he lowered his personal best time by an incredible 8 minutes. It's amazing what can happen when you get your training program and your mind focused and headed in the same direction.

» *Highly Effective Training Races*

A race is a work of art that people can look at and be affected by in as many ways as they're capable of understanding.
—STEVE PREFONTAINE

A great marathon preparation program can benefit from the proper type and number of training races. Unfortunately, many athletes race too much or too little. Or they time their training races in a way that hurts their marathon performance more than helps it.

Many athletes make the common mistake of believing they can "race themselves" into shape. This strategy is full of risk and is an extremely inefficient way to build the type of fitness needed for the marathon. This is especially true for the older athlete, who has less room for error in a training approach.

Adriana Nelson, world-class marathoner
101 Degrees West

Running a bunch of 5Ks does not prepare you to run a fast marathon. In fact, running a bunch of half marathons will not prepare you to run a fast marathon. Some athletes just love to race, and they deceive themselves into believing that frequent racing will benefit their marathon preparation. What they are actually doing is squeezing out many of the key training sessions they should be doing to prepare for their marathon.

The Three Magic Bullets sessions are at the core of a great marathon preparation plan. After a certain point, the more of these an athlete skips in order to race, the less effective his marathon preparation plan becomes. Sometimes an athlete's response is to complete the Three Magic Bullets sessions each week plus a race. This is just plain overdoing it and highly risky for injury. Not only will your races be subpar, but your training efforts will be, too. The athlete who attempts this type of approach will end up discouraged and rundown. Remember that proper rest and recovery are part of the marathon success equation.

Yet a great marathon preparation plan can benefit from the right races at the right time. Combined with the proper training, these specifically targeted races can prove the icing on the cake of an optimal training plan.

How many of these races should an athlete do? What are optimal race distances? When should they be scheduled relative to the date of the marathon? How should other training be built around these races? Answering any one of these questions incorrectly may mean the difference between achieving your marathon goal or not. Unfortunately, many athletes blow their big marathon for this exact reason many weeks before they even get to the race.

In general, we suggest between one and three training races in a sixteen-week marathon preparation phase. The best type of tune-up race for most marathoners is a half marathon scheduled in the eleven- to fourteen-week time frame of a sixteen-week marathon training program. In addition to the race being a great confidence builder, a properly scheduled half marathon training race can achieve the following:

- Confirm progress toward your marathon goal. Your race time will help you to determine if you are on track to achieve your marathon time goal.

- Be an opportunity for a marathon dress rehearsal. You can practice your pre-race routine, your pre-race and race fueling and hydration, your warm-up routine, and your race clothing.

- Provide a fun and motivating break from your regular training routine.

- Prepare for the physical and mental stress of actual racing.

TO CONFIRM PROGRESS TOWARD YOUR MARATHON GOAL

Let's first discuss how your performance in a practice half marathon can help you to know if your marathon training is on track. There is a fairly reliable rule of thumb conversion factor ratio that can be applied to your half marathon time to estimate your full marathon time. The conversion factor ratio is 2.1 to 1.0. We have used this factor with athletes for decades and have found it to be very helpful both in projecting marathon times and tracking progress toward an athlete's marathon goal.

Here is an example of how to use the 2.1 conversion factor ratio:

Current Half Marathon Time x 2.1 = Estimated Full Marathon Time

So if you are looking to run a 3:30 marathon, you would want to get very close to a time of 1:40 in your half marathon training race. Here's why:

3:30 = 210 minutes
210 minutes / 2.1 = 100 minutes
100 minutes = 1:40

Following is a chart with the conversions of popular full marathon goals to half marathon times based on a factor of 2.1.

MARATHON TIME	HALF MARATHON TIME
2:45	1:18:34
3:00	1:25.43
3:15	1:32.51
3:30	1:40.00
3:45	1:47.09
4:00	1:54.17
4:15	2:01.26
4:30	2:08.34
4:45	2:15.43
5:00	2:22.51

Your half marathon time does not have to be precisely as charted for you to know that you're on the right track, because the marathon training cycle has not yet been completed, especially the taper portion, but at least the times should be close. How close? Generally we find that you can be encouraged about your progress toward your marathon goal if your half marathon time gets you to your marathon time with at least a 2.05 conversion ratio.

So, in the above example, if your goal is to run a 3:30 marathon, in weeks 11 through 14 you should run a half marathon in a time of at least 1:42.26, if not the 1:40 as indicated in the chart above (3:30 [210 minutes] / 2.05 = 1:42.26 [102 minutes and 26 seconds]).

TO PROVIDE A DRESS REHEARSAL FOR YOUR MARATHON

Another important benefit of the half marathon training race is as a dress rehearsal for your marathon. The race provides a great opportunity to pretest many aspects of your marathon in an actual race situation. You should practice the same pre-race routine leading up to the race, the same sleeping and eating patterns, the same race morning routine, the same race warm-up, the same pre-race and race fueling and hydration, and even the same race clothing and shoes. Not only will your dress rehearsal allow you to identify any flaws in your plan and provide you with an opportunity to correct them prior to your marathon, but it will also give you greater confidence for your marathon and a real "been there, done that" positive attitude about it.

Additional tip: If possible, you should select a half marathon with similar topography to the marathon you are training for.

TO PROVIDE A FUN AND MOTIVATING BREAK FROM TRAINING

Another reason to include a half marathon as part of your marathon training is that it's fun and motivating. All training and no racing can get a little dull sometimes. A couple of properly placed practice races can add fun to your training and also serve as an ongoing motivator.

Your training may start to feel stale if your marathon is still five or six weeks away, but if you have a half marathon coming up in two weeks, you are likely to be a lot more focused on your training. In this way training races can help sustain a high motivation level throughout your sixteen-week marathon training phase.

TO PREPARE FOR THE PHYSICAL AND MENTAL STRESS OF RACING

An additional value of a half marathon training race is to help prepare the athlete for the physical and mental stress of racing. Why wait until race day to experience the nervousness and possibly self-imposed pressures of an actual race? By including a half marathon in your plan, you have an opportunity to experience and conquer this challenge well in advance of the big day.

Also, it's good to experience what a 100 percent effort feels like on a fairly long race. This is hard to replicate in training, and nothing really feels quite like a race other than a race. We want to show up the morning of our marathon with a "been there, done that" attitude, and the proper half marathon training races will help us to do that.

5Ks AND 10Ks

So we have said a half marathon training race can be helpful in the eleven- to fourteen-week period of the preparation phase, but what about additional training races? Our suggestion would be to consider one or two shorter races in the 5K to 10K range during the five- to eleven-week phase of a sixteen-week marathon training program. Personally we prefer to do just one race like this, but for those who like to race more often, two are definitely doable.

Similar to the rule of thumb conversion guidelines for the half marathon, there are also conversion factor ratios for both the 5K and the 10K. These can be helpful in the earlier weeks of our training to indicate if we are on track. But they are far less meaningful than the half marathon conversions for two primary reasons:

- The shorter the distances, the less accurate the results are in predicting marathon performance.

- The greater the number of weeks in advance of the marathon, the less accurate the results are in predicting marathon performance.

The rough conversion factors for the 5K and 10K are approximately 9.73 and 4.64, respectively.

Following is a chart with conversions of popular full marathon goals to 5K and 10K times based on the above conversion factors:

MARATHON TIME	5K	10K	HALF MARATHON
2:45	16:57	35:34	1:18:34
3:00	18:30	38:47	1:25:43
3:15	20:02	42:01	1:32:51
3:30	21:35	45:15	1:40:00
3:45	23:07	48:29	1:47:09
4:00	24:40	51:43	1:54:17
4:15	26:12	54:57	2:01:26
4:30	27:44	58:11	2:08:34
4:45	29.17	61:25	2:15:43
5:00	30.50	64:39	2:22:51

Remember, for the reasons discussed earlier, results from these shorter races are less meaningful than results from a half marathon, so they should be viewed in the proper context, along with all your other training results.

WHAT ABOUT TUNE-UP RACES LONGER THAN A HALF MARATHON?

We are often asked by athletes if races longer than a half marathon can be beneficial in preparing for a marathon. Races of 30K (18.6 miles) and 20 miles are available to athletes. Generally, racing these longer distances as part of our marathon preparation is a risky strategy. If we race these distances at a 100 percent effort, or time them too close to our actual marathon, there is a chance we will not recover fully for the marathon and "leave our best performance in training." We have seen many athletes do this over the years. They race a longer distance shortly before their marathon and never quite recover in time for their target race. They end up feeling flat on race day, unable to have the type of performance they had been on track to accomplish.

We have had success with some athletes doing longer races, however, if their pacing approach is correct and the timing of the race is optimal in terms of their marathon. The best strategy to use with these races is not to race them all out. Instead just focus on holding your Target Marathon Pace for either the 30K or 20-miler. What we have found is that if an athlete can hold his marathon pace for 18.6 to 20 miles in a racing situation while not fully tapered, he can hold it for 26.2 miles when he is fully tapered.

When combined with other factors, this is further confirmation for the athlete of his ability to maintain his Target Marathon Pace for an entire marathon. This confirmation is in addition to our discussion in Chapter 1 about how you can use the results of your TMB training sessions to confirm your ability to achieve your marathon time goal, including your ability to maintain your Target Marathon Pace for up to 80 minutes in your Marathon Pacing Sessions, which of course is a training, not a racing, situation.

If approached in this way, doing one of these longer races can be beneficial. By holding Target Marathon Pace for such a long distance when she's not tapered, the athlete receives a great shot of confidence that she can handle that same pace in her marathon when she is tapered. Secondly, since the athlete did not have to make a 100 percent effort to maintain her marathon pace for the shorter distance, she will be able to recover more quickly and be fresh, rested, and ready to go in time for the marathon.

Timing is the other major consideration with the 30K to 20-miler. For it to work as intended, it's best that the race occur three to four weeks prior to the marathon. This way very little peak training remains following the race, leaving the athlete with plenty of time to recover from the effort during his taper.

If an athlete is going to build a 30K or 20-miler into his sixteen-week marathon preparation phase, our suggestion is that he does not also run a half marathon. As mentioned before, we don't want to over-race. The 30K or 20-miler would replace the half marathon, not be in addition to it. We want to hit just the right blend of training and racing to achieve our best marathon form.

ADDITIONAL TIPS FOR PRACTICE RACES

» The "Nine-Day Guideline"

None of these practice races should be within nine days of the other; a minimum of two weeks between races is optimal. This is especially true for the forty-plus athlete. Following this guideline will help you to recover more fully, stay fresher both mentally and physically, and avoid getting run-down during the training process.

One possible good race schedule may be something like the following:

Week 6: 5K
Week 8: 10K
Week 12: Half Marathon
Week 16: Marathon

The above races all fall within the suggested time range for the respective race differences, there is a nice progression in race distances, and the races are all spaced apart by at least two weeks.

>> The "Drop Back" Long Run Week

As you learned in Chapter 1, once the Long Runs build up to their maximum duration, they begin to alternate "long and longer" every two weeks. For example, once the Long Run reaches 22 miles, the following week it will drop back to 18 miles. The next week it will revert to 22 miles, returning the next week to 18 miles. All the sixteen-week marathon training programs in Chapter 5 have this type of "long and longer" alternating pattern for the Long Runs in the peak training weeks.

If possible, it's best to schedule your training races longer than 10K for the weeks in which you have the "drop back" Long Run. In the example above, this would mean scheduling races for the weeks with the maximum 18-mile Long Runs, rather than the weeks in which you have the maximum 22-mile Long Runs.

Does this mean that if your race falls on the same day as your Long Run you can just skip it? No. If after your race you feel 100 percent healthy, we suggest that following a short break you complete whatever time or distance remains of the Long Run scheduled for that week as part of your cooldown. For example, if you do your half marathon training race on the day you have a maximum 18-mile Long Run scheduled, you should still try to push your total mileage for the day to your maximum 18-mile target.

So your warm-up, race, and cooldown may look as follows:

Pre-race easy warm-up: 1.0 mile
Half marathon race: 13.1 miles
Extended easy cooldown: 3.9 miles
Total combined mileage: 18.0 miles

Warm-up

The following suggested warm-up routine for these practice races should be about 10 to 15 minutes in duration and should begin 20 to 25 minutes before the actual race start time:

Jog easy for 3 to 5 minutes
Complete 5 x 30-second easy pickups @ 30-second easy jog
Jog easy for another 2 to 5 minutes

You should complete your warm-up routine about 10 minutes before the scheduled race start time, so you have time to find your place in the starting area and relax for a moment before the race begins.

Cooldown

After completing the race we suggest you continue to walk for 3 to 10 minutes as you cool down and have some energy drink to help rehydrate and begin the recovery process. Then you should ease into a very easy 5- to 10-minute recovery jog. As per the above, if the tune-up race was a substitution for a Long Run, you may extend your recovery jog and use this opportunity to complete the total distance for your scheduled run for the day.

Mini Taper

When you do substitute a practice race for your Long Run, you should also convert the day before into a mini taper day. In addition to resting, fueling, and hydrating well on the day before (just as you will on the day prior to your marathon), we suggest also substituting an easy 30-minute Z1 run in the morning, to replace whatever session was on the training schedule for that day.

Other Possible Training Schedule Adjustments

In addition to substituting the mini taper before the practice race, you should also eliminate the next scheduled Higher-Intensity Repeat day after the race. You should do a run for the total distance planned for that day of the training schedule, but it should be done at a moderate aerobic effort, with no Higher-Intensity Repeats. This is because the practice race itself has replaced the need for the Higher-Intensity Repeats, and to do them a couple of days after the race would be overdoing it. This risks negating the benefits of the training race and also increases the chances of injury.

Keep the above tips and suggestions in mind when selecting pre-marathon tune-up races. If you make your selections well, you will be able to better prepare for your marathon and also more accurately track your progress toward your marathon goal.

Dr. Tracie Brown is a forensic psychologist and lives in Los Angeles.

From the time she was a child her father was an avid runner, but it was not until after turning forty that Tracie became an active road racer herself. She was motivated to make this change in her life as a recovering alcoholic and significantly overweight.

She literally hit the ground running, and after only a couple of years she lost seventy-five pounds and qualified for the Boston Marathon using the program in the first edition of this book.

After she did so, we started coaching Tracie directly to help her to take her performances to the next level. Again, Dr. Brown was very successful, setting significant new personal records in the marathon, half marathon, and 10K.

Tracie's dad and running inspiration passed away at the age of ninety-three in late 2015. Although sad, it was a blessing that her dad could experience the joy of Tracie's success before his passing. Tracie dedicated her race a couple of months later to her dad. He must have been smiling while looking down from above as Tracie once again lowered her half marathon personal record, despite the very challenging terrain of the Carlsbad, California, course.

Then, three months later, Tracie amazingly did it again. She lowered her marathon personal record by another 4 minutes at the Boston Marathon. Despite the fact that Boston is not usually considered a "PR course," Tracie made it look easy.

Tracie commented, "I'm grateful that he passed his passion for fitness on to me. One of my greatest memories when I was very young is him letting us kids jog alongside him for a few miles on a Sunday and have my mom pick us up so that he could finish his workout. All three of us will be running Marine Corps in his memory."

One of those three will be Hugh, Tracie's brother, who also recently got back into road racing. He has his work cut out for him after a recent hip replacement, but with the inspiration of both his father and sister, Hugh is a good bet to achieve his goal. And when he does, a joyful father will be proudly watching from above.

» Your Perfect Marathon Training Plan

We are different, in essence, from other men. If you want to win something, run 100 meters. If you want to experience something, run a marathon.

—EMIL ZÁTOPEK

In this chapter, we will present five specific sixteen-week marathon training programs. After reading this chapter and the remainder of this book, and considering all of the variables, you will be ready to select the sixteen-week program that is best for you.

Before we introduce the actual programs, however, we will cover a number of important training approaches and philosophies that will help you to choose a marathon training program and get the most out of whichever one you select.

TRAIN IN TIME, NOT MILES

One of the most effective time-management tools for a runner is to train in time, not in miles. While we can estimate how long an 8-mile run will take, due to numerous factors—how we feel that day, weather conditions, topography, traffic, etc.—we can easily be off in our estimate. So instead of going for an 8-mile run, consider going for a 60-minute run. You can schedule it in your calendar just like any appointment. It removes all of the guesswork and results in much more time-efficient training.

This change is often tough for many long-term runners because they are so accustomed to thinking of their runs in terms of distance, not time. But give it a try. You will be glad you did.

Besides the time-management advantage, it also makes it much easier to select your running route. When we used to travel a lot, we were always driving around mapping out courses whenever we arrived in a new place. This is a big waste of time and totally unnecessary. Now we tend to run simple out-and-back courses. For a 60-minute run, we run for 30 minutes—making up the course as we go—and then we turn around and run back the same way. It's simple, efficient, and a fun way to explore a new city or country you are visiting.

We also found it to be a difficult transition when we first switched from distance to time many years ago. But as a result of making this change, our training has since been much more time-efficient. We also get a kick out of it when someone asks us how many miles we ran today and we answer back, with a smile, "Seventy-five minutes."

Now the vast majority of our coached athletes train by time, not miles. With the exception of some specific pacing work, the training plans presented in this chapter are based on a time, rather than a mileage, approach to efficient training.

HEART-RATE TRAINING

Heart-rate training is the most effective way to maximize your training time and get the most out of every training minute. After training hundreds and hundreds of endurance athletes over the years, we can think of no single training element that has led to greater performance breakthroughs than effective heart-rate training.

With all the talk about heart-rate monitors, and all the athletes you see out there training with them, you would think this is something that is used and understood by the vast majority of runners. But it is not. The reality is that few athletes train by heart rate, and of those who do, many don't do it correctly.

So many athletes have come to us for coaching over the years, and when they describe their current approach to training, we can see that they have not used heart-rate training at all. We are usually pretty excited to hear this, because almost without exception, we know these athletes will be able to improve a great deal.

The reality is that most athletes don't train hard enough on their "hard days," and they train too hard on their "easy days." All of their training gets locked into a fairly small heart-rate range in the middle. This type of training is not only inefficient, but it also leads to performance stagnation and then inevitably to mental burnout and even injury. It becomes "junk training," and who has time for that? The good news is, however, that if a lot of what you are now doing is "junk training," then it means that you may have a lot of untapped potential, just waiting to be unleashed.

As we said at the start of this book, we will not focus on a lot of complicated scientific theories and technical talk. The purpose of this book is to tell you exactly how you need to train and what you need to know to accomplish your marathon goals. Having said that, we will offer a brief explanation of what is behind effective heart-rate training.

» Aerobic vs. Anaerobic

The body's two main energy systems are the following:

- **Aerobic Energy System:** An energy system that utilizes oxygen and stored fat to power muscle activity. This system can support activity for prolonged periods of time, as stored fat and oxygen are available in almost endless supply. Even a very lean marathoner with a body-fat percentage in the single digits has enough stored fat to run several marathons back-to-back.

- **Anaerobic Energy System:** An energy system that utilizes glycogen (stored sugar) to power muscle activity. This system cannot support activity for long periods of time, as the body stores sugar in relatively limited quantities.

While both of these energy systems work at the same time, the ratio of the two systems changes as the level of activity changes. The intensity of our training activity determines the ratio at which we are drawing from each system. The higher the intensity, the more anaerobic the activity. The lower the intensity, the more aerobic the activity.

Heart rate is an excellent indicator of where we are in the spectrum of aerobic and anaerobic ratios. At lower heart rates, the mix is more aerobic. At higher heart rates, the mix is more anaerobic. As our effort level and heart rate increase, the mix becomes more anaerobic.

The important point to understand is that the benefit of an effective heart-rate training program is that you are training at the proper intensity level at the right time, which serves to develop both your aerobic and anaerobic systems.

As mentioned earlier, the vast majority of athletes train at the wrong intensity most of the time, resulting in highly ineffective training—often to the point of being "junk training." The most successful marathoners understand that they need to put out a very big effort on their "hard days," and they need to restrain their effort to a moderate level on "easy days." A good heart-rate training program has the athlete in the proper Heart Rate Zone at the right time, resulting in highly effective training.

» Estimating Your Heart Rate Zones

The most accurate way to determine your maximum heart rate and heart-rate training zones is to be tested. Many universities and fitness centers offer these testing services at a relatively modest cost. If it is not possible to have testing done, there are also various low-tech methods for estimating your maximum heart rate. The most popular of these is the "220 Minus Your Age" method. You simply subtract your age from 220 and this provides an estimate of your maximum heart rate (MHR).

Women tend to have a slightly higher maximum heart rate then men. Subtracting a woman's age from 226 often provides a more accurate result. So, for women, we suggest the "226 Minus Your Age" method.

For example, according to this method a fifty-year-old male's maximum heart rate would be estimated at 170 beats per minute (220 – 50 = 170 MHR). While this estimate is pretty close to being correct for the majority of fifty-year-olds, we usually encourage our coached athletes to race a 5K with a heart-rate monitor and see what their maximum heart rate was for the race. This is usually a very good indication of maximum heart rate.

Once you have figured out your maximum heart rate, we can use it to determine the four training zones we'll use with the marathon training plans included in this chapter:

- Zone 4: 90–95 percent of MHR (anaerobic training)

- Zone 3: 86–89 percent of MHR (middle zone)

- Zone 2: 75–85 percent of MHR (higher-end aerobic training)

- Zone 1: 65–74 percent of MHR (lower-end aerobic training)

For the fifty-year-old marathoner with a 170 MHR, Heart Rate Zones would be:

- Z4: 90–95 percent of 170 MHR = 153 to 162 beats per minute (BPM)

- Z3: 86–89 percent of 170 MHR = 146 to 152 BPM

- Z2: 75–85 percent of 170 MHR = 128 to 145 BPM

- Z1: 65–74 percent of 170 MHR = 111 to 127 BPM

SELECTING YOUR MARATHON TIME GOAL

Many athletes want to select a good time goal for their marathon. Typically the best marathon goal for an athlete is one that is possible, but will take some work to achieve. Challenging but achievable; most athletes find this to be the most motivating type of goal. But what is the best way to establish this? It is especially difficult to do if this will be your first marathon.

Following are the criteria we usually work through with many of our coached athletes when helping them to determine their marathon goal:

- Past marathon times

- Past race times for other distances

- Three Magic Bullets training results

- Lactate threshold testing results

≫ Past Marathon Times

The first thing we look at is the athlete's previous best marathon time and perhaps her most recent marathon time. As an example, if an athlete recorded a personal best time of 3:30 about a year ago and training has been going very well since, selecting a time of about 10 to 15 seconds per mile faster is usually a good motivating goal. It's challenging, but if all goes well during the sixteen-week training program and on race day, it is achievable. Since a 3:30 equates to an average of about 8 minutes per mile, an average of 15 seconds faster would be about 7:45 minutes per mile, which equates to a marathon time goal of about 3:23.

≫ Past Race Times for Other Distances

If the athlete has never raced a marathon before, or has not raced one recently, we may want to take a look at the athlete's recent results at other race distances. In Chapter 4, we presented conversion ratios for the 5K, 10K, and half marathon. These conversion ratios help us to estimate a runner's marathon time based on her time at one of these shorter distances.

For example, if an athlete has never raced a marathon but has recently raced a half marathon in a time of 1:37, we can apply the 2.1 conversion ratio to get an estimate of the equivalent marathon time, as follows:

1:37 = 97 minutes
97 minutes x 2.1 = 203 minutes = 3:23

So a marathon goal of around 3:23 may be appropriate for this athlete.

» Three Magic Bullets Training Results

An athlete's pacing results while doing the Three Magic Bullets sessions will actually help confirm his ability to maintain a certain pace for the marathon. Because of this, the TMB sessions are useful for either determining what your marathon goal should be or double-checking your predetermined goal based on one of the other criteria discussed above.

As explained in detail in Chapter 1, if you can maintain a specific Target Marathon Pace for all of your Marathon Pacing Sessions, and if you can run 30 seconds or more faster per mile than this pace for your Higher-Intensity Repeats, and if you can maintain a pace of 30 to 60 seconds slower than this pace for your Long Runs, then you are typically fit enough to maintain this target pace for an entire marathon, if all else is equal.

» Lactate Threshold Testing Results

As we said earlier, one of our goals for this book was not to focus on a lot of complicated scientific theories and technical talk. After decades of coaching hundreds and hundreds of athletes, we know that this is not what the vast majority of athletes want. They want straightforward and easily understandable steps to achieving their goals. So this fourth option is a nice-to-have but definitely not a need-to-have criterion.

Lactate threshold is the heart rate at which lactate accumulates at a faster rate in the muscles than your body can clear it. Lactate is produced in our bodies when performing physical activity. Our bodies have the ability to clear this lactate up to a point. But after crossing the lactate threshold, the lactate accumulates at a faster rate than it can be cleared. This accumulation has a negative impact on the muscles' ability to perform.

Ideally our optimal marathon pace needs to be slightly below this point. If you have lactate testing done and know your lactate threshold, then this information can be used along with the three criteria above to double-check your Target Marathon Pace and marathon goal time. However, lactate testing is not necessary, and the first three criteria alone are more than sufficient to determine your goal.

TRAINING PROGRAMS

Following are five sixteen-week marathon training plans. These programs are designed to show the athlete exactly what his training should be for each and every day over the sixteen-week period in order to achieve his individual marathon goals.

The same plan that helps an athlete in his teens, twenties, and thirties to achieve his goals may very well lead to injury for the athlete in his forties, fifties, and sixties. The plans presented in this chapter take this into account.

Each plan will be explained so that the reader may select the one that fits his or her profile, experience level, age, health, and time goals. Take all of these factors into account when you make your selection. Once you have chosen the program you feel is best suited to you, share its specifics with your doctor so that he knows exactly what your plans are and is 100 percent comfortable with you running a marathon.

Additional note on pacing: The examples included in the following discussions of Training Programs A through E refer to Target Marathon Pace. As we will discuss in "Pacing" in Chapter 11, you may want to consider setting your Target Marathon Pace 5 to 7 seconds faster than the pace necessary to achieve your marathon time goal. These 5 to 7 seconds per mile will add up to provide a 2- to 3-minute time cushion for your marathon time goal.

EXPLANATION OF TRAINING PLAN ABBREVIATIONS

Following are explanations for the abbreviations used in the sixteen-week marathon training plans:

Z1 = Heart Rate Zone 1

Z2 = Heart Rate Zone 2

Z3 = Heart Rate Zone 3

Z4 = Heart Rate Zone 4

hr = heart rate

HR = Hill Repeats

PU = Easy pickups: Increase run pace by about 10 percent for 1 minute, followed by a 1-minute easy jog. Repeat this sequence for a total of 5 repetitions.

45-minute Z1 to Z2 = Run for 45 minutes keeping heart rate within Z1 and Z2.

1:15-hour Z2 = Run for 1 hour and 15 minutes keeping heart rate within Z2.

1:15-hour Z2 (@ 10 minutes, 8 x 400 Z4 @ 200 jog) = Higher-Intensity Repeat session. Start this 1-hour, 15-minute session by running in Z2 for 10 minutes. (Note: Allow yourself a few minutes to ease in and gradually increase your heart rate into Z2.) Then, at the 10-minute point, run 400 meters in Z4, followed by an easy 200-meter recovery jog. Repeat this sequence a total of 8 times. Use whatever time is left of the total 1 hour and 15 minutes in Z2.

400 = 400 meters = 0.25 mile

600 = 600 meters = 0.375 mile

800 = 800 meters = 0.5 mile

1200 = 1,200 meters = 0.75 mile

1600 = 1,600 meters = 1.0 mile

2000 = 2,000 meters = 1.25 miles

1:30-hour Z2 (@ 55 minutes, insert 30-minute MPS) = Marathon Pacing Session. Start this 1-hour, 30-minute session by running in Z2 for 55 minutes. (Note: Allow yourself a few minutes to ease in and gradually increase your heart rate into Z2). Then, at the 55-minute point, increase your pace to your Target Marathon Pace for 30 minutes. While running at your Target Marathon Pace, you can expect to see your heart rate in or around Z3. Use whatever time is left of the total 1 hour and 30 minutes in Z2.

Lesser of 2:30-hour Z1 to Z2 or 18 miles = Long Run session. Run within Z1 and Z2 for either 2 hours and 30 minutes or 18 miles, whichever of the two occurs first.

Rest Day/Slide Day = Either take the day off, or if you missed a workout during the week, use this as a catch-up day. When doing so, it's better to keep all training sessions in order and simply slide them forward by one day.

XT = Cross-training sessions (e.g., elliptical, pool running, cross-country skiing, etc. See Chapter 3 for more cross-training ideas).

TRAINING PROGRAM A: RUN ONLY: ADVANCED

Program A: Run-Only: Advanced is for the experienced and advanced marathoner who is in perfect health, able to run six times per week without injury, and is targeting a marathon finishing time of 3:30 or faster. The athlete who selects this program has raced several marathons before and now wants to build on his past race performances with a new personal best time for the marathon.

This program includes the Three Magic Bullets run sessions, plus three weekly moderate aerobic runs. Program A is best suited for athletes who fit Level 1 in the Free Miles Training Hierarchy (see Chapter 3). Since Level 1 athletes are less prone to injury, this program includes Hill Repeats. Tips on how to further customize this program to fit your individual needs are presented later in this chapter.

The Z4 repeats in the Higher-Intensity Repeat sessions should be at a pace 30 seconds or more faster than your Target Marathon Pace. The Marathon Pacing Sessions should be at your Target Marathon Pace, and your Long Runs should be 30 to 60 seconds slower than your Target Marathon Pace. The longest of the Long Runs in this program peaks at the lesser of 3:10 hours or 22 miles.

Following are two examples of how to calculate the proper paces and distances:

≫ Athlete #1

- 7:00 minutes per mile Target Marathon Pace (equates to about a 3:03 marathon)

- Higher-Intensity Repeat pace = 6:30 minutes per mile or faster (i.e., 30 seconds or more faster than Target Marathon Pace)

- Marathon Pacing Session pace = 7:00 minutes per mile

- Long Run pace = 7:30 to 8:00 minutes per mile (i.e., 30 to 60 seconds slower than Target Marathon Pace)

- Long Run distance for the peak Long Runs is the lesser of 3:10 hours or 22 miles. Depending on what pace the athlete selects within the range of 7:30 to 8:00 minutes per mile, he will complete his maximum 22-mile run in 2:45 hours to 2:56 hours. (Note: 7:30 minutes per mile x 22 miles = 2:45 hours, and 8:00 minutes per mile x 22 miles = 2:56 hours.)

≫ Athlete #2:

- 8:00 minutes per mile Target Marathon Pace (equates to about a 3:29 marathon)

- Higher-Intensity Repeat pace = 7:30 minutes per mile or faster (i.e., 30 seconds or more faster than Target Marathon Pace)

- Marathon Pacing Session pace = 8:00 minutes per mile

- Long Run pace = 8:30 to 9:00 minutes per mile (i.e., 30 to 60 seconds slower than Target Marathon Pace)

- Long Run distance for the peak Long Runs is the lesser of 3:10 hours or 22 miles. Depending on what pace the athlete selects within the range of 8:30 to 9:00 minutes per mile, he will complete his maximum 22-mile run in 3:07 hours to 3:10 hours. (Note: 8:30 minutes per mile x 22 miles = 3:07 hours, and 9:00 minutes per mile x 22 miles = 3:18, but the maximum time suggested is 3:10 hours.)

Total weekly training hours start at 4:00 hours in Week 1 and build to a peak of 8:55 to 9:40 hours in the plan's most challenging weeks.

An athlete should not begin this program unless he has gradually and safely worked up to 4 hours per week of moderate running in the four to eight weeks prior.

TRAINING PROGRAM A: RUN ONLY: ADVANCED

(Part 1: Weeks 1–8) (Note: See sidebar on pages 63–64 for definitions of all abbreviations.)

DAY/ WEEK	Week 1 Sessions	Week 2 Sessions	Week 3 Sessions	Week 4 Sessions	Week 5 Sessions	Week 6 Sessions	Week 7 Sessions	Week 8 Sessions
Mon	45 min Z1 to Z2	45 min Z1 to Z2	60 min Z1 to Z2	60 min Z2	60 min Z2	60 min Z2	60 min Z2	60 min Z2
Tues	45 min Z2	45 min Z2	60 min Z2	60 min Z2	1:15 hr Z2	1:15 hr Z2	1:15 hr Z2 (@ 10 min, insert PU)	1:15 hr Z2 (@ 10 min, 8 x 800 Z4 @ 200 jog)
Wed	Off	45 min Z1 to Z2	45 min Z1 to Z2	60 min Z2	60 min Z2	60 min Z2	60 min Z2	60 min Z2
Thur	45 min Z2	45 min Z2	60 min Z2	1:15 hr Z2	1:15 hr Z2	1:15 hr Z2	1:15 hr Z2 (@ 60 min, insert PU)	1:30 hr Z2 (@ 55 min, insert 30 min MPS)
Fri	45 min Z1 to Z2	45 min Z1 to Z2	45 min Z1 to Z2	60 min Z2	60 min Z2	60 min Z2	60 min Z2	60 min Z2
Sat	60 min Z1 to Z2	1:15 hr Z1 to Z2	1:30 hr Z1 to Z2	1:45 hr Z1 to Z2	2:00 hr Z1 to Z2	The lesser of 2:30 hr Z1 to Z2 or 18 miles	The lesser of 3:10 hr Z1 to Z2 or 22 miles	The lesser of 2:30 hr Z1 to Z2 or 18 miles

Sun	Rest Day/ Slide Day	Rest Day/ Slide Day	Rest Day/ Slide Day	Rest Day/ Slide Day	Rest Day/ Slide Day	Rest Day/ Slide Day	Rest Day/ Slide Day	Rest Day/ Slide Day
Total	4:00 hr Run	5:00 hr Run	6:00 hr Run	7:00 hr Run	7:30 hr Run	8:00 hr Run	8:40 hr Run	8:15 hr Run

TRAINING PROGRAM A: RUN ONLY: ADVANCED

(Part 2: Weeks 9–16)

DAY/ WEEK	Week 9 Sessions	Week 10 Sessions	Week 11 Sessions	Week 12 Sessions	Week 13 Sessions	Week 14 Sessions	Week 15 Sessions	Week 16 Sessions
Mon	60 min Z2	60–75 min Z2	60–75 min Z2	60–75 min Z2	60–75 min Z2	60 min Z2	60 min Z2	45 min Z2
Tues	1:15 hr Z2 (@ 10 min, 10 x 2 min Z4 HR @ jog back down)	1:15 hr Z2 (@ 10 min, 4 x 1600 Z4 @ 400 jog)	1:15 hr Z2 (@ 10 min, 10 x 2.5 min Z4 HR @ jog back down)	1:15 hr Z2 (@ 10 min, 4 x 2000 Z4 @ 400 jog)	1:15 hr Z2 (@ 10 min, 10 x 3 min Z4 HR @ jog back down)	1:15 hr Z2 (@ 10 min, 3 x 1600 Z4 @ 400 jog)	60 min Z2 (@ 10 min, 4 x 800 Z4 @ 400 jog)	45 min Z2 (@ 10 min, insert PU)
Wed	60 min Z2	60–75 min Z2	60–75 min Z2	60–75 min Z2	60–75 min Z2	60 min Z2	45 min Z2	Off
Thur	1:30 hr Z2 (@ 45 min, insert 40 min MPS)	1:30 hr Z2 (@ 35 min, insert 50 min MPS)	1:30 hr Z2 (@ 25 min, insert 60 min MPS)	1:30 hr Z2 (@ 15 min, insert 70 min MPS)	1:30 hr Z2 (@ 5 min, insert 80 min MPS)	1:15 hr Z2 (@ 30 min, insert 40 min MPS)	60 min Z2 (@ 35 min, insert 20 min MPS)	40 min Z1 (@ 10 min, insert PU)
Fri	60 min Z2	60–75 min Z2	60–75 min Z2	60–75 min Z2	60–75 min Z2	60 min Z2	45 min Z2	20 min Z1 easy (in a.m.)
Sat	The lesser of 3:10 hr Z1 to Z2 or 22 miles	The lesser of 2:30 hr Z1 to Z2 or 18 miles	The lesser of 3:10 hr Z1 to Z2 or 22 miles	The lesser of 2:30 hr Z1 to Z2 or 18 miles	The lesser of 3:10 hr Z1 to Z2 or 22 miles	2:00 hr Z1 to Z2	60 min Z1 to Z2	Marathon!
Sun	Rest Day/ Slide Day	Rest Day/ Slide Day	Rest Day/ Slide Day	Rest Day/ Slide Day	Rest Day/ Slide Day	Rest Day/ Slide Day	Rest Day/ Slide Day	Rest Day/ Slide Day
Total	8:55 hr Run	8:15–9:00 hr Run	8:55–9:40 hr Run	8:15–9:00 hr Run	8:55–9:40 hr Run	7:30 hr Run	5:30 hr Run	2:30 hr + Marathon

TRAINING PROGRAM B: RUN ONLY: 3:30-PLUS

Program B: Run-Only: 3:30-Plus is for the experienced marathoner who is in perfect health, able to run five times per week without injury, and, based on reasonable expectations and past performances, has a marathon time goal of over 3:30 hours. It is also for the first-time marathoner who is in perfect health and able to run five times per week without injury.

This program includes the Three Magic Bullets run sessions, plus two weekly moderate aerobic runs. There are also two Rest Day/Slide Days, one of which can be used as an optional moderate aerobic cross-training day of up to 60 minutes, at the athlete's option.

Like Program A, Program B is best suited for athletes who fit Level 1 in the Free Miles Training Hierarchy (see Chapter 3). Since Level 1 athletes are less prone to injury, this program includes Hill Repeats. Tips on how to further customize this program to fit your individual needs are presented later in this chapter.

The Z4 repeats in the Higher-Intensity Repeat sessions should be at a pace 30 seconds or more faster than your Target Marathon Pace. The Marathon Pacing Sessions should be at your Target Marathon Pace, and the Long Runs should be 30 to 60 seconds slower than your Target Marathon Pace. The longest of the Long Runs in this program peaks at the lesser of 3:30 hours or 22 miles.

Following are two examples of how to calculate the proper paces and distances:

» Athlete #1

- 9:00 minutes per mile Target Marathon Pace (equates to about a 3:56 marathon)

- Higher-Intensity Repeat pace = 8:30 minutes per mile or faster (i.e., 30 seconds or more faster than Target Marathon Pace)

- Marathon Pacing Session pace = 9:00 minutes per mile

- Long Run pace = 9:30 to 10:00 minutes per mile (i.e., 30 to 60 seconds slower than Target Marathon Pace)

- Long Run distance for the peak Long Runs is the lesser of 3:30 hours or 22 miles. Depending on what pace the athlete selects within the range of 9:30 to 10:00 minutes per mile, he will complete his maximum 22-mile run in 3:29 hours to 3:30 hours. (Note: 9:30 minutes per mile x 22 miles = 3:29 hours, and 10:00 minutes per mile x 22 miles = 3:40, but the maximum time suggested is 3:30 hours.)

» Athlete #2

- 10:00 minutes per mile Target Marathon Pace (equates to about a 4:22 marathon)

- Higher-Intensity Repeat pace = 9:30 minutes per mile or faster (i.e., 30 seconds or more faster than Target Marathon Pace)

- Marathon Pacing Session pace = 10:00 minutes per mile

- Long Run pace = 10:30 to 11:00 minutes per mile (i.e., 30 to 60 seconds slower than Target Marathon Pace)

- Long Run distance for the peak Long Runs is the lesser of 3:30 hours or 22 miles. Since this athlete reaches 3:30 hours prior to 22 miles, no matter what pace the athlete selects within the range of 10:30 to 11:00 minutes per mile, he will conclude his Long Run at 3:30. (Note: 10:30 minutes per mile x 22 miles = 3.51 hours, and 11:00 minutes per mile x 22 miles = 4:02 hours.) We do not recommend training runs of longer than 3:30 hours.

Total weekly training hours start at 3:30 hours in Week 1 and build to a peak of 8:15 hours in the plan's most challenging weeks.

An athlete should not begin this program unless he has gradually and safely worked up to 3.5 hours per week of moderate running in the four to eight weeks prior.

TRAINING PROGRAM B: RUN ONLY: 3:30-PLUS
(Part 1: Weeks 1–8) (Note: See sidebar on pages 63–64 for definitions of all abbreviations.)

DAY/ WEEK	Week 1 Sessions	Week 2 Sessions	Week 3 Sessions	Week 4 Sessions	Week 5 Sessions	Week 6 Sessions	Week 7 Sessions	Week 8 Sessions
Mon	30 min Z1 to Z2	30 min Z1 to Z2	30 min Z1 to Z2	45 min Z2	45 min Z2	45 min Z2	45 min Z2	45 min Z2
Tues	45 min Z2	45 min Z2	60 min Z2	60 min Z2	60 min Z2	60 min Z2	60 min Z2 (@ 10 min, insert PU)	60 min Z2 (@ 10 min, 8 x 800 Z4 @ 200 jog)
Wed	Rest Day/ Slide Day	Rest Day/ Slide Day	Rest Day/ Slide Day	Rest Day/ Slide Day	Rest Day/ Slide Day	Rest Day/ Slide Day	Rest Day/ Slide Day	Rest Day/ Slide Day
Thur	45 min Z2	45 min Z2	60 min Z2	60 min Z2	60 min Z2	60 min Z2	60 min Z2 (@ 45 min, insert PU)	60 min Z2 (@ 25 min, insert 30 min MPS)
Fri	30 min Z1 to Z2	30 min Z1 to Z2	30 min Z1 to Z2	45 min Z2	45 min Z2	45 min Z2	45 min Z2	45 min Z2
Sat	60 min Z1 to Z2	1:15 hr Z1 to Z2	1:30 hr Z1 to Z2	1:45 hr Z1 to Z2	2:00 hr Z1 to Z2	2:15 hr Z1 to Z2	2:30 hr Z1 to Z2	The lesser of 2:45 hr Z1 to Z2 or 18 miles
Sun	Rest Day/ Slide Day	Rest Day/ Slide Day	Rest Day/ Slide Day	Rest Day/ Slide Day	Rest Day/ Slide Day	Rest Day/ Slide Day	Rest Day/ Slide Day	Rest Day/ Slide Day
Total	3:30 hr Run	3:45 hr Run	4:30 hr Run	5:15 hr Run	5:30 hr Run	5.45 hr Run	6:00 hr Run	6:15 hr Run

TRAINING PROGRAM B: RUN ONLY: 3:30-PLUS
(Part 2: Weeks 9–16)

DAY/ WEEK	Week 9 Sessions	Week 10 Sessions	Week 11 Sessions	Week 12 Sessions	Week 13 Sessions	Week 14 Sessions	Week 15 Sessions	Week 16 Sessions
Mon	45 min Z2	60 min Z2	60 min Z2	60 min Z2	60 min Z2	60 min Z2	45 min Z2	45 min Z2
Tues	60 min Z2 (@ 10 min, 10 x 2 min Z4 HR @ jog back down)	1:15 hr Z2 (@ 10 min, 4 x 1600 Z4 @ 400 jog)	1:15 hr Z2 (@ 10 min, 10 x 2.5 min Z4 HR @ jog back down)	1:15 hr Z2 (@ 10 min, 4 x 2000 Z4 @ 400 jog)	1:15 hr Z2 (@ 10 min, 10 x 3 min Z4 HR @ jog back down)	60 min Z2 (@ 10 min, 2 x 1600 Z4 @ 400 jog)	45 min Z2 (@ 10 min, 2 x 800 Z4 @ 400 jog)	45 min Z2 (@ 10 min, insert PU)
Wed	Rest Day/ Slide Day	Rest Day/ Slide Day	Rest Day/ Slide Day	Rest Day/ Slide Day	Rest Day/ Slide Day	Rest Day/ Slide Day	Rest Day/ Slide Day	Rest Day/ Slide Day
Thur	60 min Z2 (@ 15 min, insert 40 min MPS)	1:15 hr Z2 (@ 20 min, insert 50 min MPS)	1:15 hr Z2 (@ 10 min, insert 60 min MPS)	1:30 hr Z2 (@ 15 min, insert 70 min MPS)	1:30 hr Z2 (@ 5 min, insert 80 min MPS)	60 min Z2 (@ 15 min, insert 40 min MPS)	45 min Z2 (@ 20 min, insert 20 min MPS)	40 min Z1 (@ 10 min, insert PU)
Fri	45 min Z2	60 min Z2	60 min Z2	60 min Z2	60 min Z2	60 min Z2	45 min Z2	20 min Z1 easy run (in a.m.)
Sat	The lesser of 3:30 hr Z1 to Z2 or 22 miles	The lesser of 2:45 hr Z1 to Z2 or 18 miles	The lesser of 3:30 hr Z1 to Z2 or 22 miles	The lesser of 2:45 hr Z1 to Z2 or 18 miles	The lesser of 3:30 hr Z1 to Z2 or 22 miles	2:00 hr Z1 to Z2	60 min Z1 to Z2	Marathon!
Sun	Rest Day/ Slide Day	Rest Day/ Slide Day	Rest Day/ Slide Day	Rest Day/ Slide Day	Rest Day/ Slide Day	Rest Day/ Slide Day	Rest Day/ Slide Day	Rest Day/ Slide Day
Total	7:00 hr Run	7:15 hr Run	8:00 hr Run	7:30 hr Run	8:15 hr Run	6:00 hr Run	4:00 hr Run	2:30 hr + Marathon

TRAINING PROGRAM C: RUN/ CROSS-TRAIN: ADVANCED

Program C: Run/Cross-Train: Advanced is for the advanced marathoner who is in very good health, but due to either past injury history or future preventative reasons would prefer to run only three times per week, and cross-train (e.g., elliptical, pool running, cross-country skiing, etc.) three times per week, and who has a marathon time goal of 3:30 hours or faster. The athlete who selects this program has raced several marathons before and now wants to build on his past race performances with a new personal best time for the marathon.

This program includes the Three Magic Bullets run sessions, plus three weekly moderate aerobic cross-training sessions. See Chapter 3 to help select the best cross-training activities for you.

Program C is best suited for athletes who fit Level 2 or Level 3 in the Free Miles Training Hierarchy (see Chapter 3). The only difference is that Level 2 athletes will be substituting Transition Sessions for some or all of the moderate aerobic cross-training sessions. Since Level 2 and Level 3 athletes are more prone to injury, Hill Repeats are not suggested or included in this training program. However, if you want to add them you will find tips on how to further customize this program to fit your individual needs later in this chapter.

The Z4 repeats in the Higher-Intensity Repeat sessions should be at a pace 30 seconds or more faster than your Target Marathon Pace. The Marathon Pacing Sessions should be at your Target Marathon Pace, and your Long Runs should be 30 to 60 seconds slower than your Target Marathon Pace. The longest of the Long Runs in this program peaks at the lesser of 3:10 hours or 22 miles.

Following are two examples of how to calculate the proper paces and distances:

» Athlete #1

- 7:00 minutes per mile Target Marathon Pace (equates to about a 3:03 marathon)

- Higher-Intensity Repeat pace = 6:30 minutes per mile or faster (i.e., 30 seconds or more faster than Target Marathon Pace)

- Marathon Pacing Session pace = 7:00 minutes per mile

- Long Run pace = 7:30 to 8:00 minutes per mile (i.e., 30 to 60 seconds slower than Target Marathon Pace)

- Long Run distance for the peak Long Runs is the lesser of 3:10 hours or 22 miles. Depending on what pace the athlete selects within the range of 7:30 to 8:00 minutes per mile, he will complete his maximum 22-mile run in 2:45 hours to 2:56 hours (Note: 7:30 minutes per mile x 22 miles = 2:45 hours, and 8:00 minutes per mile x 22 miles = 2:56 hours.)

» Athlete #2

- 8:00 minutes per mile Target Marathon Pace (equates to about a 3:29 marathon)

- Higher-Intensity Repeat pace = 7:30 minutes per mile or faster (i.e., 30 seconds or more faster than Target Marathon Pace)

- Marathon Pacing Session pace = 8:00 minutes per mile

- Long Run pace = 8:30 to 9:00 minutes per mile (i.e., 30 to 60 seconds slower than Target Marathon Pace)

- Long Run distance for the peak Long Runs is the lesser of 3:10 hours or 22 miles. Depending on what pace the athlete selects within the range of 8:30 to 9:00 minutes per mile, he will complete his maximum 22-mile run in 3:07 hours to 3:10 hours (Note: 8:30 minutes per mile x 22 miles = 3:07 hours, and 9:00 minutes per mile x 22 miles = 3:18, but the maximum time suggested is 3:10 hours.)

Total weekly training hours start at 4:00 hours (2:30 hours running and 1:30 hours cross-training) in Week 1 and build to a peak of 8:55 to 9:40 hours (5:55 hours running and 3:00 to 3:45 hours cross-training) in the plan's most challenging weeks.

An athlete should not begin this program unless he has gradually and safely worked up to 4 hours per week of combined moderate running and cross-training in the four to eight weeks prior.

TRAINING PROGRAM C: RUN/CROSS-TRAIN: ADVANCED

(Part 1: Weeks 1–8) (Note: See sidebar on pages 63–64 for definitions of all abbreviations. All sessions are run sessions unless identified as XT = cross-training sessions.)

DAY/ WEEK	Week 1 Sessions	Week 2 Sessions	Week 3 Sessions	Week 4 Sessions	Week 5 Sessions	Week 6 Sessions	Week 7 Sessions	Week 8 Sessions
Mon	45 min Z1 to Z2 XT	45 min Z1 to Z2 XT	60 min Z1 to Z2 XT	60 min Z1 to Z2 XT	60 min Z1 to Z2 XT	60 min Z1 to Z2 XT	60 min Z1 to Z2 XT	60 min Z1 to Z2 XT
Tues	45 min Z2	45 min Z2	60 min Z2	60 min Z2	1:15 hr Z2	1:15 hr Z2	1:15 hr Z2 (@ 10 min, insert PU)	1:15 hr Z2 (@ 10 min, 10 x 600 Z4 @ 200 jog)
Wed	Off	45 min Z1 to Z2 XT	45 min Z1 to Z2 XT	60 min Z1 to Z2 XT	60 min Z1 to Z2 XT	60 min Z1 to Z2 XT	60 min Z1 to Z2 XT	60 min Z1 to Z2 XT
Thur	45 min Z2	45 min Z2	60 min Z2	1:15 hr Z2	1:15 hr Z2	1:15 hr Z2	1:15 hr Z2 (@ 60 min, insert PU)	1:30 hr Z2 (@ 55 min, insert 30 min MPS)
Fri	45 min Z1 to Z2 XT	45 min Z1 to Z2 XT	45 min Z1 to Z2 XT	60 min Z1 to Z2 XT	60 min Z1 to Z2 XT	60 min Z1 to Z2 XT	60 min Z1 to Z2 XT	60 min Z1 to Z2 XT
Sat	60 min Z1 to Z2	1:15 hr Z1 to Z2	1:30 hr Z1 to Z2	1:45 hr Z1 to Z2	2:00 hr Z1 to Z2	The lesser of 2:30 hr Z1 to Z2 or 18 miles	The lesser of 3:10 hr Z1 to Z2 or 22 miles	The lesser of 2:30 hr Z1 to Z2 or 18 miles

Sun	Rest Day/ Slide Day	Rest Day/ Slide Day	Rest Day/ Slide Day	Rest Day/ Slide Day	Rest Day/ Slide Day	Rest Day/ Slide Day	Rest Day/ Slide Day	Rest Day/ Slide Day
Total	1:30 hr XT 2:30 hr Run 4:00 hr Total	2:15 hr XT 2:45 hr Run 5:00 hr Total	2:30 hr XT 3:30 hr Run 6:00 hr Total	3:00 hr XT 4:00 hr Run 7:00 hr Total	3:00 hr XT 4:30 hr Run 7:30 hr Total	3:00 hr XT 5:00 hr Run 8:00 hr Total	3:00 hr XT 5:40 hr Run 8:40 hr Total	3:00 hr XT 5:15 hr Run 8:15 hr Total

TRAINING PROGRAM C: RUN/CROSS-TRAIN: ADVANCED
(Part 2: Weeks 9–16)

DAY/ WEEK	Week 9 Sessions	Week 10 Sessions	Week 11 Sessions	Week 12 Sessions	Week 13 Sessions	Week 14 Sessions	Week 15 Sessions	Week 16 Sessions
Mon	60 min Z1 to Z2 XT	60 min Z1 to Z2 XT	60–75 min Z1 to Z2 XT	60–75 min Z1 to Z2 XT	60–75 min Z1 to Z2 XT	60 min Z1 to Z2 XT	60 min Z1 to Z2 XT	45 min Z1 to Z2 XT
Tues	1:15 hr Z2 (@ 10 min, 16 x 400 Z4 @ 100 jog)	1:15 hr Z2 (@ 10 min, 4 x 1600 Z4 @ 400 jog)	1:15 hr Z2 (@ 10 min, 8 x 800 Z4 @ 200 jog)	1:15 hr Z2 (@ 10 min, 4 x 2000 Z4 @ 400 jog)	1:15 hr Z2 (@ 10 min, 7 x 1200 Z4 @ 400 jog)	1:15 hr Z2 (@ 10 min, 3 x 1600 Z4 @ 400 jog)	60 min Z2 (@ 10 min, 4 x 800 Z4 @ 400 jog)	45 min Z2 (@ 10 min, insert PU)
Wed	60 min Z1 to Z2 XT	60 min Z1 to Z2 XT	60–75 min Z1 to Z2 XT	60–75 min Z1 to Z2 XT	60–75 min Z1 to Z2 XT	60 min Z1 to Z2 XT	45 min Z1 to Z2 XT	Off
Thur	1:30 hr Z2 (@ 45 min, insert 40 min MPS)	1:30 hr Z2 (@ 35 min, insert 50 min MPS)	1:30 hr Z2 (@ 25 min, insert 60 min MPS)	1:30 hr Z2 (@ 15 min, insert 70 min MPS)	1:30 hr Z2 (@ 5 min, insert 80 min MPS)	1:15 hr Z2 (@ 30 min, insert 40 min MPS)	60 min Z2 (@ 35 min, insert 20 min MPS)	40 min Z1 (@ 10 min, insert PU)
Fri	60 min Z1 to Z2 XT	60 min Z1 to Z2 XT	60–75 min Z1 to Z2 XT	60–75 min Z1 to Z2 XT	60–75 min Z1 to Z2 XT	60 min Z1 to Z2 XT	45 min Z1 to Z2 XT	20 min Z1 easy run (in a.m.)
Sat	The lesser of 3:10 hr Z1 to Z2 or 22 miles	The lesser of 2:30 hr Z1 to Z2 or 18 miles	The lesser of 3:10 hr Z1 to Z2 or 22 miles	The lesser of 2:30 hr Z1 to Z2 or 18 miles	The lesser of 3:10 hr Z1 to Z2 or 22 miles	2:00 hr Z1 to Z2	60 min Z1 to Z2	Marathon!
Sun	Rest Day/ Slide Day	Rest Day/ Slide Day	Rest Day/ Slide Day	Rest Day/ Slide Day	Rest Day/ Slide Day	Rest Day/ Slide Day	Rest Day/ Slide Day	Rest Day/ Slide Day
Total	3:00 hr XT 5:55 hr Run 8:55 hr Total	3:00 hr XT 5:15 hr Run 8:15 hr Total	3:00–3:45 XT 5:55 hr Run 8:55–9:40 Total	3:00–3:45 XT 5:15 hr Run 8:15–9:00 Total	3:00–3:45 XT 5:55 hr Run 8:55–9:40 Total	3:00 hr XT 4:30 hr Run 7:30 hr Total	2:30 hr XT 3:00 hr Run 5:30 hr Total	2:30 hr + Marathon

TRAINING PROGRAM D: RUN/ CROSS-TRAIN: 3:30-PLUS

Program D: Run/Cross-Train: 3:30-Plus is for the experienced marathoner who is in good health, but due to either past injury history or future preventative reasons would prefer to run only three times per week and cross-train (e.g., elliptical, pool running, cross-country skiing, etc.) two times per week. Based on reasonable expectations and past performances, this athlete has a marathon time goal of over 3:30 hours. It is also for the first-time marathoner who is in good health, but due to the same reasons would prefer to run only three times per week and cross-train two times per week.

This program includes the Three Magic Bullets run sessions, plus two weekly moderate aerobic cross-train sessions. There are also two Rest Day/Slide Days, one of which can be used as an optional moderate aerobic cross-training day of up to 60 minutes, at the athlete's option.

Like Program C, Program D is best suited for athletes who fit Level 2 or Level 3 in the Free Miles Training Hierarchy (see Chapter 3). Just as with Program C, the only difference is that the Level 2 athletes will be substituting Transition Sessions for some or all of the moderate aerobic cross-training sessions. Since Level 2 and Level 3 athletes are more prone to injury, Hill Repeats are not suggested or included in this training program. However, if you want to add them you will find tips on how to further customize this program to fit your individual needs later in this chapter.

The Z4 repeats in the Higher-Intensity Repeat sessions should be at a pace 30 seconds or more faster than your Target Marathon Pace. The Marathon Pacing Sessions should be at your Target Marathon Pace, and your Long Runs should be 30 to 60 seconds slower than your Target Marathon Pace. The longest of the Long Runs in this program peaks at the lesser of 3:30 hours or 22 miles.

Following are two examples of how to calculate the proper paces and distances:

❯❯ Athlete #1

- 9:00 minutes per mile Target Marathon Pace (equates to about a 3:56 marathon)

- Higher-Intensity Repeat pace = 8:30 minutes per mile or faster (i.e., 30 seconds or more faster than Target Marathon Pace)

- Marathon Pacing Session pace = 9:00 minutes per mile

- Long Run pace = 9:30 to 10:00 minutes per mile (i.e., 30 to 60 seconds slower than Target Marathon Pace)

- Long Run distance for the peak Long Runs is the lesser of 3:30 hours or 22 miles. Depending on what pace the athlete selects within the range of 9:30 to 10:00 minutes per mile, he will complete his maximum 22-mile run in 3:29 hours to 3:30 hours (Note: 9:30 minutes per mile x 22 miles = 3:29 hours, and 10:00 minutes per mile x 22 miles = 3:40, but the maximum time suggested is 3:30 hours.)

» Athlete #2

- 10:00 minutes per mile Target Marathon Pace (equates to about a 4:22 marathon)

- Higher-Intensity Repeat pace = 9:30 minutes per mile or faster (i.e., 30 seconds or more faster than Target Marathon Pace)

- Marathon Pacing Session pace = 10:00 minutes per mile

- Long Run pace = 10:30 to 11:00 minutes per mile (i.e., 30 to 60 seconds slower than Target Marathon Pace)

- Long Run distance for the peak Long Runs is the lesser of 3:30 hours or 22 miles. Since this athlete reaches 3:30 hours prior to 22 miles, no matter what pace the athlete selects within the range of 10:30 to 11:00 minutes per mile, he will conclude his Long Run at 3:30 hours. (Note: 10:30 minutes per mile x 22 miles = 3:51 hours, and 11:00 minutes per mile x 22 miles = 4:02 hours.) We do not recommend training runs of longer than 3:30 hours.

Total weekly training hours start at 3:30 hours (2:30 hours running and 1:00 hour of cross-training) in Week 1 and build to a peak of 8:15 hours (6:15 hours running and 2:00 hours of cross-training) in the plan's most challenging weeks.

An athlete should not begin this program unless he has gradually and safely worked up to 3.5 hours per week of combined moderate running and cross-training in the four to eight weeks prior.

TRAINING PROGRAM D: RUN/CROSS-TRAIN: 3:30-PLUS

(Part 1: Weeks 1–8) (Note: See sidebar on pages 63–64 for definitions of all abbreviations.
All sessions are run sessions unless identified as XT = cross-training sessions.)

DAY/WEEK	Week 1 Sessions	Week 2 Sessions	Week 3 Sessions	Week 4 Sessions	Week 5 Sessions	Week 6 Sessions	Week 7 Sessions	Week 8 Sessions
Mon	30 min Z1 to Z2 XT	30 min Z1 to Z2 XT	30 min Z1 to Z2 XT	45 min Z1 to Z2 XT	45 min Z1 to Z2 XT	45 min Z1 to Z2 XT	45 min Z1 to Z2 XT	45 min Z1 to Z2 XT
Tues	45 min Z2	45 min Z2	60 min Z2	60 min Z2	60 min Z2	60 min Z2	60 min Z2 (@ 10 min, insert PU)	60 min Z2 (@ 10 min, 8 x 600 Z4 @ 200 jog)
Wed	Rest Day/ Slide Day	Rest Day/ Slide Day	Rest Day/ Slide Day	Rest Day/ Slide Day	Rest Day/ Slide Day	Rest Day/ Slide Day	Rest Day/ Slide Day	Rest Day/ Slide Day
Thur	45 min Z2	45 min Z2	60 min Z2	60 min Z2	60 min Z2	60 min Z2	60 min Z2 (@ 45 min, insert PU)	60 min Z2 (@ 25 min, insert 30 min MPS)
Fri	30 min Z1 to Z2 XT	30 min Z1 to Z2 XT	30 min Z1 to Z2 XT	45 min Z1 to Z2 XT	45 min Z1 to Z2 XT	45 min Z1 to Z2 XT	45 min Z1 to Z2 XT	45 min Z1 to Z2 XT
Sat	60 min Z1 to Z2	1:15 hr Z1 to Z2	1:30 hr Z1 to Z2	1:45 hr Z1 to Z2	2:00 hr Z1 to Z2	2:15 hr Z1 to Z2	2:30 hr Z1 to Z2	The lesser of 2:45 hr Z1 to Z2 or 18 miles
Sun	Rest Day/ Slide Day	Rest Day/ Slide Day	Rest Day/ Slide Day	Rest Day/ Slide Day	Rest Day/ Slide Day	Rest Day/ Slide Day	Rest Day/ Slide Day	Rest Day/ Slide Day
Total	60 min XT 2:30 hr Run 3:30 hr Total	60 min XT 2:45 hr Run 3:45 hr Total	60 min XT 3:30 hr Run 4:30 hr Total	1:30 hr XT 3:45 hr Run 5:15 hr Total	1:30 hr XT 4:00 hr Run 5:30 hr Total	1:30 hr XT 4:15 hr Run 5:45 hr Total	1:30 hr XT 4:30 hr Run 6:00 hr Total	1:30 hr XT 4:45 hr Run 6:15 hr Total

TRAINING PROGRAM D: RUN/CROSS-TRAIN: 3:30-PLUS

(Part 2: Weeks 9–16)

DAY/WEEK	Week 9 Sessions	Week 10 Sessions	Week 11 Sessions	Week 12 Sessions	Week 13 Sessions	Week 14 Sessions	Week 15 Sessions	Week 16 Sessions
Mon	45 min Z1 to Z2 XT	60 min Z1 to Z2 XT	60 min Z1 to Z2 XT	60 min Z1 to Z2 XT	60 min Z1 to Z2 XT	60 min Z1 to Z2 XT	45 min Z1 to Z2 XT	45 min Z1 to Z2 XT
Tues	60 min Z2 (@ 10 min, 12 x 400 Z4 @ 100 jog)	1:15 hr Z2 (@ 10 min, 3 x 1600 Z4 @ 400 jog)	1:15 hr Z2 (@ 10 min, 6x 800 Z4 @ 200 jog)	1:15 hr Z2 (@ 10 min, 3 x 2000 Z4 @ 400 jog)	1:15 hr Z2 (@ 10 min, 6 x 1200 Z4 @ 400 jog)	60 min Z2 (@ 10 min, 2 x 1600 Z4 @ 400 jog)	45 min Z2 (@ 10 min, 2 x 800 Z4 @ 200 jog)	45 min Z2 (@ 10 min, insert PU)

Wed	Rest Day/ Slide Day	Rest Day/ Slide Day	Rest Day/ Slide Day	Rest Day/ Slide Day	Rest Day/ Slide Day	Rest Day/ Slide Day	Rest Day/ Slide Day	Rest Day/ Slide Day
Thur	60 min Z2 (@ 15 min, insert 40 min MPS)	1:15 hr Z2 (@ 20 min, insert 50 min MPS)	1:15 hr Z2 (@ 10 min, insert 60 min MPS)	1:30 hr Z2 (@ 15 min, insert 70 min MPS)	1:30 hr Z2 (@ 5 min, insert 80 min MPS)	60 min Z2 (@ 15 min, insert 40 min MPS)	45 min Z2 (@ 20 min, insert 20 min MPS)	40 min Z1 (@ 10 min, insert PU)
Fri	45 min Z1 to Z2 XT	60 min Z1 to Z2 XT	60 min Z1 to Z2 XT	60 min Z1 to Z2 XT	60 min Z1 to Z2 XT	60 min Z1 to Z2 XT	45 min Z1 to Z2 XT	20 min Z1 easy run (in a.m.)
Sat	The lesser of 3:30 hr Z1 to Z2 or 22 miles	The lesser of 2:45 hr Z1 to Z2 or 18 miles	The lesser of 3:30 hr Z1 to Z2 or 22 miles	The lesser of 2:45 hr Z1 to Z2 or 18 miles	The lesser of 3:30 hr Z1 to Z2 or 22 miles	2:00 hr Z1 to Z2	60 min Z1 to Z2	Marathon!
Sun	Rest Day/ Slide Day	Rest Day/ Slide Day	Rest Day/ Slide Day	Rest Day/ Slide Day	Rest Day/ Slide Day	Rest Day/ Slide Day	Rest Day/ Slide Day	Rest Day/ Slide Day
Total	1:30 hr XT 5:30 hr Run 7:00 hr Total	2:00 hr XT 5:15 hr Run 7:15 hr Total	2:00 hr XT 6:00 hr Run 8:00 hr Total	2:00 hr XT 5:30 hr Run 7:30 hr Total	2:00 hr XT 6:15 hr Run 8:15 hr Total	2:00 hr XT 4:00 hr Run 6:00 hr Total	1:30 hr XT 2:30 hr Run 4:00 hr Total	45 min XT 1:45 hr Run 2:30 + Marathon

TRAINING PROGRAM E: CROSS-TRAIN/ BARE BONES RUN

Program E: Cross-Train/Bare Bones Run is for the experienced marathoner or the first-timer who is in good health, but due to either past injury history or future preventative reasons would prefer to base his marathon preparation in cross-training (e.g., elliptical, pool running, cross-country skiing, etc.), with only a minimal amount of actual running.

This program includes the Three Magic Bullets sessions, but only the Marathon Pacing Session is a run-only workout. The Higher-Intensity Repeat session is completed using a cross-training option, and the Long Run is split between 50 percent running and 50 percent cross-training. In addition to the Three Magic Bullets sessions, there are two other moderate aerobic cross-training days and two Rest Day/Slide Days, one of which can be used as an optional moderate aerobic cross-training day of up to 60 minutes.

Program E is best suited for athletes who fit Level 4 in the Free Miles Training Hierarchy (see Chapter 3). Tips on how to further customize this program to fit your individual needs are presented later in this chapter.

Since the Z4 repeats in the Higher-Intensity Repeat sessions will be completed using one of the cross-training options, they will be strictly based on heart rate and timed intervals. The higher-intensity portion will always be in Z3 to Z4, and the moderate portion will always be in Z1 to Z2.

The first half of each Long Run will be completed using one of the cross-training options and the second half will be completed with actual running. The duration of the 50/50 Cross-Train/Long Runs should be the amount of time indicated in the training schedule for athletes with a projected marathon finishing time of 3:30 hours or more. If your finishing time is faster than 3:30 hours, your total time should not exceed your projected finishing time, and the cross-training and run portions should be evenly divided.

The following example demonstrates how to calculate the time of your Long Runs if your projected finishing time is more than 3:30 hours. Training Program E indicates a 3:30-hour Cross-Train/Long Run session as follows: 1:45-hour Z1 to Z2 XT + 1:45-hour Z1 to Z2 run. If this athlete's projected marathon time is 3:00 hours, he should reduce the times of this workout as follows: 1:30-hour Z1 to Z2 XT + 1:30-hour Z1 to Z2 run.

The next example demonstrates how to calculate the proper paces for the Three Magic Bullets sessions:

» Athlete #1

- 9:00 minutes per mile Target Marathon Pace (equates to about a 3:56 marathon)

- Higher-Intensity Z3 to Z4 interval pace = These sessions will be completed using a cross-training option, so no running pace applies. Sessions will be based on heart rate and timed intervals.

- Marathon Pacing Session pace = 9:00 minutes per mile

- Long Run pace = The run portion of the Long Runs will have a pace between 9:30 to 10:00 minutes per mile (i.e., 30 to 60 seconds slower than Target Marathon Pace). The cross-training portion will be based on heart rate (Z1 to Z2) and time.

Total weekly training hours start at 3:30 hours (1:15 hours running and 2:15 hours cross-training) in Week 1 and build to a peak of 8:15 hours (3:15 hours running and 5:00 hours cross-training) in the plan's most challenging weeks.

An athlete should not begin this program unless he has gradually and safely worked up to 3.5 hours per week of combined moderate running and cross-training in the four to eight weeks prior.

TRAINING PROGRAM E: CROSS-TRAIN/BARE BONES RUN

(Part 1: Weeks 1–8) (Note: See sidebar on pages 63–64 for definitions of all abbreviations.)

DAY/ WEEK	Week 1 Sessions	Week 2 Sessions	Week 3 Sessions	Week 4 Sessions	Week 5 Sessions	Week 6 Sessions	Week 7 Sessions	Week 8 Sessions
Mon	30 min Z1 to Z2 XT	30 min Z1 to Z2 XT	30 min Z1 to Z2 XT	45 min Z1 to Z2 XT	45 min Z1 to Z2 XT	45 min Z1 to Z2 XT	45 min Z1 to Z2 XT	45 min Z1 to Z2 XT
Tues	45 min Z1 to Z2 XT	45 min Z1 to Z2 XT	60 min Z1 to Z2 XT	60 min Z1 to Z2 XT	60 min Z1 to Z2 XT	60 min Z1 to Z2 XT	60 min Z1 to Z2 XT (@ 10 min, insert PU)	60 min Z1 to Z2 XT (@ 10 min, 3 x 1 min Z3 to Z4 @ 30 sec easy)
Wed	Rest Day/ Slide Day	Rest Day/ Slide Day	Rest Day/ Slide Day	Rest Day/ Slide Day	Rest Day/ Slide Day	Rest Day/ Slide Day	Rest Day/ Slide Day	Rest Day/ Slide Day
Thur	45 min Z2 run	45 min Z2 run	60 min Z2 run	60 min Z2 run	60 min Z2 run	60 min Z2 run	60 min Z2 run (@ 45 min, insert PU)	60 min Z2 run (@ 25 min, insert 30 min MPS)
Fri	30 min Z1 to Z2 XT	30 min Z1 to Z2 XT	30 min Z1 to Z2 XT	45 min Z1 to Z2 XT	45 min Z1 to Z2 XT	45 min Z1 to Z2 XT	45 min Z1 to Z2 XT	45 min Z1 to Z2 XT
Sat	30 min Z1 to Z2 XT + 30 min Z1 to Z2 run*	37.5 min Z1 to Z2 XT + 37.5 min Z1 to Z2 run*	45 min Z1 to Z2 XT + 45 min Z1 to Z2 run*	52.5 min Z1 to Z2 XT + 52.5 min Z1 to Z2 run*	60 min Z1 to Z2 XT + 60 min Z1 to Z2 run*	67.5 min Z1 to Z2 XT + 67.5 min Z1 to Z2 run*	75 min Z1 to Z2 XT + 75 min Z1 to Z2 run*	1:22.5 Z1 to Z2 XT + 1:22.5 Z1 to Z2 run*
Sun	Rest Day/ Slide Day	Rest Day/ Slide Day	Rest Day/ Slide Day	Rest Day/ Slide Day	Rest Day/ Slide Day	Rest Day/ Slide Day	Rest Day/ Slide Day	Rest Day/ Slide Day
Total	2:15 hr XT 1:15 hr Run 3:30 hr Total	2:22 hr XT 1:22 hr Run 3:45 hr Total	2:45 hr XT 1:45 hr Run 4:30 hr Total	3:22 hr XT 1:52 hr Run 5:15 hr Total	3:30 hr XT 2:00 hr Run 5:30 hr Total	3:37 hr XT 2:07 hr Run 5:45 hr Total	3:45 hr XT 2:15 hr Run 6:00 hr Total	3:52 hr XT 2:22 hr Run 6:15 hr Total

*Note: These Saturday Long Runs are split between cross-training and running.

TRAINING PROGRAM E: CROSS-TRAIN/BARE BONES RUN
(Part 2: Weeks 9–16)

DAY/ WEEK	Week 9 Sessions	Week 10 Sessions	Week 11 Sessions	Week 12 Sessions	Week 13 Sessions	Week 14 Sessions	Week 15 Sessions	Week 16 Sessions
Mon	45 min Z1 to Z2 XT	60 min Z1 to Z2 XT	60 min Z1 to Z2 XT	60 min Z1 to Z2 XT	60 min Z1 to Z2 XT	60 min Z1 to Z2 XT	45 min Z1 to Z2 XT	45 min Z1 to Z2 XT
Tues	60 min Z1 to Z2 XT (@ 10 min, 3 x 2 min Z3 to Z4 @ 1 min easy)	1:15 hr Z1 to Z2 XT (@ 10 min, 3 x 3 min Z3 to Z4 @ 1.5 min easy)	1:15 hr Z1 to Z2 XT (@ 10 min, 3 x 4 min Z3 to Z4 @ 2 min easy)	1:15 hr Z1 to Z2 XT (@ 10 min, 3 x 5 min Z3 to Z4 @ 2.5 min easy)	1:15 hr Z1 to Z2 XT (@ 10 min, 3 x 6 min Z3 to Z4 @ 3 min easy)	60 min Z1 to Z2 XT (@ 10 min, 2 x 5 min Z3 to Z4 @ 2.5 min easy)	45 min Z1 to Z2 XT (@ 10 min, 2 x 3 min Z3 to Z4 @ 1.5 min easy)	45 min Z1 to Z2 XT (@ 10 min, insert PU)
Wed	Rest Day/ Slide Day	Rest Day/ Slide Day	Rest Day/ Slide Day	Rest Day/ Slide Day	Rest Day/ Slide Day	Rest Day/ Slide Day	Rest Day/ Slide Day	Rest Day/ Slide Day
Thur	60 min Z2 run (@ 15 min, insert 40 min MPS)	1:15 hr Z2 run (@ 20 min, insert 50 min MPS)	1:15 hr Z2 run (@ 10 min, insert 60 min MPS)	1:30 hr Z2 run (@ 15 min, insert 70 min MPS)	1:30 hr Z2 run (@ 5 min, insert 80 min MPS)	60 min Z2 run (@ 15 min, insert 40 min MPS)	45 min Z2 run (@ 20 min, insert 20 min MPS)	40 min Z1 run (@ 10 min, insert PU)
Fri	45 min Z1 to Z2 XT	60 min Z1 to Z2 XT	60 min Z1 to Z2 XT	60 min Z1 to Z2 XT	60 min Z1 to Z2 XT	60 min Z1 to Z2 XT	45 min Z1 to Z2 XT	20 min Z1 easy run (in a.m.)
Sat	1:45 Z1 to Z2 XT + 1:45 Z1 to Z2 run*	1:22.5 Z1 to Z2 XT + 1:22.5 Z1 to Z2 run*	1:45 Z1 to Z2 XT + 1:45 Z1 to Z2 run*	1:22.5 Z1 to Z2 XT + 1:22.5 Z1 to Z2 run*	1:45 Z1 to Z2 XT + 1:45 Z1 to Z2 run*	60 min Z1 to Z2 XT + 60 min Z1 to Z2 run*	30 min Z1 to Z2 XT + 30 min Z1 to Z2 run*	Marathon!
Sun	Rest Day/ Slide Day	Rest Day/ Slide Day	Rest Day/ Slide Day	Rest Day/ Slide Day	Rest Day/ Slide Day	Rest Day/ Slide Day	Rest Day/ Slide Day	Rest Day/ Slide Day
Total	4:15 hr XT 2:45 hr Run 7:00 hr Total	4:37 hr XT 2:37 hr Run 7:15 hr Total	5:00 hr XT 3:00 hr Run 8:00 hr Total	4:37 hr XT 2:53 hr Run 7:30 hr Total	5:00 hr XT 3:15 hr Run 8:15 hr Total	4:00 hr XT 2:00 hr Run 6:00 hr Total	2:45 hr XT 1:15 hr Run 4:00 hr Total	1:30 hr XT 1:00 hr Run 2:30 + Marathon

*Note: These Saturday Long Runs are split between cross-training and running.

TRAINING PROGRAM SUBSTITUTIONS TO CONSIDER

While our five sixteen-week training programs are designed to fit a wide range of athletes, they can be further fine-tuned to the specific needs of the athlete by incorporating many of the techniques and tips from this book. Some of the most helpful substitutions are the following:

- **Transition Session Substitutions:** One popular adjustment to the marathon training programs is to use Transition Sessions to either increase or decrease the amount of running. As described in Chapter 3, "Free Running Miles," these are simply sessions that start with a cross-training activity (e.g., the elliptical machine) and then at a certain point in the session, the athlete makes a quick change into running gear (if necessary) and finishes with a run. An example of a typical 60-minute Transition Session is to use the elliptical for 45 minutes and then immediately change to running gear and go for a 15-minute run. All five training programs can either be adjusted to increase the amount of running by substituting Transition Sessions for cross-training sessions or to decrease the amount of running by substituting Transition Sessions for run sessions. Consider these options if you want to further adjust any of the programs to the amount of running time you personally feel most comfortable with.

- **Higher-Intensity Repeat Substitutions:** We talked earlier about how the Higher-Intensity Repeats are the most physically stressful sessions and that some athletes should consider using one of the suggested forms of cross-training for this workout (as suggested in Training Plan E above) or possibly skip them entirely. Another possible option is to do these sessions every other week instead of every week as in the described training plans. For example, instead of doing Higher-Intensity Repeats every week from the eighth week to the fifteenth week as presented in programs A, B, C, and D, you can do them in Weeks 8, 10, 12, and 14. Then just do a Z1 to Z2 run of the same length in Weeks 9, 11, 13, and 15. Higher-Intensity Repeat sessions are discussed in detail in Chapter 1.

- **Hill Repeat Substitutions:** Hill Repeats can also be very stressful on the body and should only be considered by those who are fully healthy and find that they rarely get injured. This is why we have only included them in Training Programs A and B. If you are using Programs C or D and feel that you are not at risk for injury, you may want to consider adding them. Our suggestion for substituting Hill Repeats into the marathon training plans is to alternate these sessions each week with the Higher-Intensity Repeat sessions, until the week in which the taper begins, at which point Hill Repeats should be discontinued. For example, do the Higher-Intensity Repeats as planned in Weeks 8, 10, 12, and 14 and substitute Hill Repeats in Weeks 9, 11, and 13. So in the even weeks (i.e., 8, 10, 12, and 14) you will be doing Higher-Intensity Repeats as presented in the training program, but in the odd weeks (i.e., 9, 11, and 13) you will be doing them as Hill Repeats. Hill Repeats are also discussed in detail in Chapter 1. If you are using Program E, we do not suggest you consider adding hill repeats.

- **Additional Cross-Train Day for Programs B, D, and E:** These three marathon training programs all have two weekly Rest Day/Slide Days. If you are working with one of these programs and find that you only need one rest day per week instead of two, you can convert one of the two Rest Day/Slide Days into a 30- to 60-minute Z1 to Z2 cross-train day.

❯❯ SCOTT BOYLES:
40-Plus Athlete Success Story

Scott Boyles, an attorney based in Wilmington, North Carolina, has two sons and has been married for more than twenty-one years. Scott started running marathons and triathlons later in life, with his first marathon in 2008 at the age of forty-two. That first marathon was in Myrtle Beach, and Scott finished in a time of 3:37.

Soon after that race Scott began a coaching relationship with us, and we of course introduced him to the Three Magic Bullets approach to marathon training. Amazingly, in his very next marathon, less than a year later, Scott took 18 minutes off his time, going 3:19 at the Disney Marathon and qualifying for the Boston Marathon for the first time.

Scott's times have improved so quickly that we suspect we have only just begun to tap his great potential. Scott credits his marathon success to having a one-on-one coaching relationship and a program focused on the Three Magic Bullets approach.

Through his training and racing success over recent years, Scott feels he is not only fitter, but has also become a much more mentally prepared, focused, and confident athlete. Of the Three Magic Bullets sessions, Scott probably least enjoys the Marathon Pacing Sessions, but he values the benefits of this workout the most. While he says these sessions can be mentally tough, Scott enjoys the challenge and views them as having been especially important to his marathon progress.

Despite all of Scott's marathon success since turning forty, expect him to be running even faster marathons for many years to come and enjoying even more success at the races.

» Your Perfect Half Marathon Training Program

The gun goes off and everything changes . . . the world changes . . . and nothing else really matters. **—PATTI SUE PLUMER**

There is more excitement and interest in the half marathon distance than ever before. According to a recent article in *Idea* magazine, "Since 2003, the half marathon has been the fastest-growing standard distance in the United States, with a 12.5% annual finisher growth rate." Total half marathon finishers in the United States eclipsed two million for the first time in 2014.

While still a worthy challenge, preparing for and racing a half marathon requires less time and affords a greater overall lifestyle balance. What most people do not realize is that training for the half marathon is much different than training for the full marathon. Simply cutting the marathon program in half, which some uninformed people might think to do, is neither a wise approach nor will optimize results.

In this chapter we present three specific training programs for the half marathon, each including the powerful training concepts and approaches presented in this book. We also provide helpful tips and advice on how best to use the half marathon and full marathon training programs together to maximize your results in both.

The half marathon is the most popular road-racing distance . . . for good reason! It's not too much . . . it's not too little . . . it's just right. Training for a marathon is absolutely doable for a busy person with family, career, and other priorities, but it may be a little more than what many people can or want to take on. And for those who do take it on, it's only a once-a-year or once-in-a-while thing.

The beauty of the half marathon is that while it is long enough and challenging enough to motivate any athlete, it is also doable with a much smaller time commitment. As you will see in the training programs presented in this chapter, an average of only about 5 or 6 hours a week is all you need.

You will also notice the half marathon training programs are twelve weeks, instead of sixteen weeks like the marathon, demonstrating how an athlete can safely prepare to race a half much more quickly. This quicker preparation time, combined with a faster recovery time, means that unlike the marathon, you can safely race several half marathons in a single year.

The other wonderful feature about the half marathon is that it is more common.

The fact that there are more of them means that you will likely find many more races closer to you. While a marathon often requires a good bit of travel and perhaps even hotel accommodations, half marathons are logistically easier.

Stated simply, the advantages of the half marathon include less training time, more frequent racing, less travel, and less overall expense. One even bigger consideration: There is a lower occurrence of injury, which is of particular value to the forty-plus athlete.

HALF MARATHON TRAINING PROGRAMS

Following are three specific half marathon training programs. The first is run-only, the second is running combined with cross-training, and the third is a "bare bones" program that prepares the athlete to run a half marathon with a minimal amount of actual running.

» *Training Program AA: Run Only*

Program AA: Run Only is for the more experienced road racer who is in perfect health and able to run six times per week without injury. The athlete who selects this program has raced at least one half marathon before and now wants to build on his past race performance with a new personal best time for the half marathon.

This program includes the two types of higher-intensity run sessions (i.e., Higher-Intensity Repeats and Higher-Intensity Inserts), plus three weekly moderate aerobic runs.

Program A is best suited for athletes who fit Level One in the Free Miles Training Hierarchy presented in Chapter 3. Since Level One athletes are less prone to injury, this program includes Hill Repeats. Tips on how to further customize this program to fit your individual needs are presented in Chapter 5.

For all ZA portions in either the Higher-Intensity Repeats Sessions and the Higher-Intensity Insert Sessions, your target pace should be your 5K equivalent pace for all efforts of less than 8 minutes and your 10K pace for all efforts greater than 8 minutes in duration. Easily determine these paces using the chart in Chapter 4. Simply use your target half marathon time and pace to identify the equivalent 5K and 10K paces. Your Long Runs should be 45 to 75 seconds slower than your Target Half Marathon Pace.

The longest of the Long Runs in this program peaks at 2:15 hours.

HALF MARATHON TRAINING PROGRAM AA: RUN ONLY

DAY/WEEK	Week 1 Sessions	Week 2 Sessions	Week 3 Sessions	Week 4 Sessions	Week 5 Sessions	Week 6 Sessions
Mon	45 min Z1 to Z2	45 min Z2	60 min Z2	60 min Z2	60 min Z2	60 min Z2
Tues	45 min Z1 to Z2	45 min Z2	45 min Z2	60 min Z2 (@10 min, insert PU)	60 min Z2 (@ 10 min, insert 16 x 200 Z4 @ 100 jog)	60 min Z2 (@ 10 min, insert 12 x 2 min Z4 HR)
Wed	Off	45 min Z2—optional	45 min Z2—optional	45 min Z2—optional	45 min Z2—optional	60 min Z2—optional
Thur	45 min Z1 to Z2	45 min Z2	45 min Z2	45 min Z2 (@ 30 min, insert PU)	60 min Z2 (@ 45 min, insert 5 min Z4)	60 min Z2 (@ 45 min, insert 7.5 min Z4)
Fri	45 min Z1 to Z2	45 min Z2	45 min Z2	45 min Z2	45 min Z2	60 min Z2
Sat	60 min Z1 to Z2	1:15 hr Z1 to Z2	1:30 hr Z1 to Z2	1:45 hr Z1 to Z2	2:00 hr Z1 to Z2	2:15 hr Z1 to Z2
Sun	Rest Day/Slide Day	Rest Day/Slide Day	Rest Day/Slide Day	Rest Day/Slide Day	Rest Day/Slide Day	Rest Day/Slide Day
Total	4:00 hrs	4:15–5:00 hrs	4:45-5:30 hrs	5:15–6:00 hrs	5:45–6:30 hrs	6:15–7:15 hrs

DAY/WEEK	Week 7 Sessions	Week 8 Sessions	Week 9 Sessions	Week 10 Sessions	Week 11 Sessions	Week 12 Sessions
Mon	60 min Z2	60 min Z2	60 min Z2	60 min Z2	60 min Z2	45 min Z2
Tues	1:15 hr Z2 (@ 10 min, insert 8 x 400 Z4 @ 100 jog)	1:15 hr Z2 (@ 10 min, insert 10 x 2.5 min Z4 HR)	1:15 hr Z2 (@ 10 min, insert 6 x 800 Z4 @ 200 jog)	1:15 hr Z2 (@ 10 min, insert 8 x 3 min Z4 HR)	1:15 hr Z2 (@ 10 min, insert 4 x 1600 Z4 @ 400 jog)	45 min Z1 to Z2 (@ 10 min, insert PU)
Wed	60 min Z2—optional	60 min Z2—optional	60 min Z2—optional	60 min Z2—optional	45 min Z2—optional	Off
Thur	60 min Z2 (@ 45 min, insert 10 min Z4)	60 min Z2 (@ 40 min, insert 12.5 min Z4)	1:15 hr Z2 (@ 55 min, insert 15 min Z4)	1:15 hr Z2 (@ 55 min, insert 15 min Z4)	1:15 hr Z2 (@ 55 min, insert 15 min Z4)	40 min Z1 to Z2 (@ 10 min, insert PU)
Fri	60 min Z2	60 min Z2	60 min Z2	60 min Z2	45 min Z2	20 min Z1, easy (in a.m.)
Sat	1:45 hr Z1 to Z2	2:15 hr Z1 to Z2	1:45 hr Z1 to Z2	2:15 hr Z1 to Z2	1:15 hr Z1 to Z2	Half Marathon!
Sun	Rest Day/Slide Day	Rest Day/Slide Day	Rest Day/Slide Day	Rest Day/Slide Day	Rest Day/Slide Day	Rest Day/Slide Day
Total	6:00–7:00 hrs	6:30–7:30 hrs	6:15–7:15 hrs	6:45–7:45 hrs	5:30–6:15 hrs	2:30 hrs + Race

» *Training Program BB: Run/Cross-Train*

Training Program BB: Run/Cross-Train is for the road racer who is in very good health, but due to either past injury history or future preventative reasons would prefer to run three times per week and cross-train (e.g., elliptical, pool running, cross-country ski, etc.) three times per week. The athlete who selects this program is either preparing to race his first half marathon, or has raced one before and now wants to build on his past race performance with a new personal best time for the half marathon.

This program includes the two types of higher-intensity run sessions (i.e., Higher-Intensity Repeats and Higher-Intensity Inserts), plus three weekly moderate cross-training sessions.

Program BB is best suited for athletes who fit Level Two or Level Three in the Free Miles Training Hierarchy presented in Chapter 3. The only difference will be that the Level Two athletes will be substituting Transition Sessions for some or all of the moderate aerobic cross-training sessions. Since Level 2 and Level 3 athletes are more prone to injury, Hill Repeats are not suggested or included in this training program. Tips on how to further customize this program to fit your individual needs are presented in Chapter 5.

For all Z4 portions in either the Higher-Intensity Repeat sessions and the Higher-Intensity Insert sessions, your target pace should be your 5K equivalent pace for all efforts of less than 8 minutes and your 10K pace for all efforts greater than 8 minutes in duration. Easily determine these paces using the chart in Chapter 4. Simply use your target half marathon time and pace to identify the equivalent 5K and 10K paces. Your Long Runs should be 45 to 75 seconds slower than your Target Half Marathon Pace.

The longest of the Long Runs in this program peaks at 2:15 hours.

HALF MARATHON TRAINING PROGRAM BB: RUN/CROSS-TRAIN

DAY/WEEK	Week 1 Sessions	Week 2 Sessions	Week 3 Sessions	Week 4 Sessions	Week 5 Sessions	Week 6 Sessions
Mon	45 min Z1 to Z2 XT	45 min Z2 XT	60 min Z2 XT	60 min Z2 XT	60 min Z2 XT	60 min Z2 XT
Tues	45 min Z1 to Z2	45 min Z2	45 min Z2	60 min Z2 (@ 10 min, insert PU)	60 min Z2 (@ 10 min, insert 16 x 200 Z4 @ 100 jog)	60 min Z2 (@ 10 min, insert 10 x 400 Z4 @ 200 jog)
Wed	Off	45 min Z2 XT—optional	45 min Z2 XT—optional	45 min Z2 XT—optional	45 min Z2 XT—optional	60 min Z2 XT—optional
Thur	45 min Z1 to Z2	45 min Z2	45 min Z2	45 min Z2 (@ 30 min, insert PU)	60 min Z2 (@ 45 min, insert 5 min Z4)	60 min Z2 (@ 45 min, insert 7.5 min Z4)
Fri	45 min Z1 to Z2 XT	45 min Z2 XT	45 min Z2 XT	45 min Z2 XT	45 min Z2 XT	60 min Z2 XT
Sat	60 min Z1 to Z2	1:15 hr Z1 to Z2	1:30 hr Z1 to Z2	1:45 hr Z1 to Z2	2:00 hr Z1 to Z2	2:15 hr Z1 to Z2
Sun	Rest Day/Slide Day	Rest Day/Slide Day	Rest Day/Slide Day	Rest Day/Slide Day	Rest Day/Slide Day	Rest Day/Slide Day
Total	1:30 hrs XT 2:30 hrs Run 4:00 hrs Total	1:30–2:15 hrs XT 2:45 hrs Run 4:15–5:00 hrs Total	1:45–2:30 hrs XT 3:00 hrs Run 4:45–5:30 hrs Total	1:45–2:30 hrs XT 3:30 hrs Run 5:15–6:00 hrs Total	1:45–2:30 hrs XT 4:00 hrs Run 5:45–6:30 hrs Total	2:00–3:00 hrs XT 4:15 hrs Run 6:15–7:15 hrs Total

DAY/WEEK	Week 7 Sessions	Week 8 Sessions	Week 9 Sessions	Week 10 Sessions	Week 11 Sessions	Week 12 Sessions
Mon	60 min Z2 XT	60 min Z2 XT	60 min Z2 XT	60 min Z2 XT	60 min Z2 XT	45 min Z2 XT
Tues	1:15 hr Z2 (@ 10 min, insert 7 x 600 Z4 @ 200 jog)	1:15 hr Z2 (@ 10 min, insert 6 x 800 Z4 @ 200 jog)	1:15 hr Z2 (@ 10 min, insert 4 x 1200 Z4 @ 300 jog)	1:15 hr Z2 (@ 10 min, insert 3 x 1600 Z4 @ 400 jog)	1:15 hr Z2 (@ 10 min, insert 6 x 800 Z4 @ 200 jog)	45 min Z1 to Z2 (@ 10 min, insert PU)
Wed	60 min Z2 XT—optional	60 min Z2 XT—optional	60 min Z2 XT—optional	60 min Z2 XT—optional	45 min Z2 XT—optional	Off
Thur	60 min Z2 (@ 45 min, insert 10 min Z4)	60 min Z2 (@ 40 min, insert 12.5 min Z4)	1:15 hr Z2 (@ 55 min, insert 15 min Z4)	1:15 hr Z2 (@ 55 min, insert 15 min Z4)	1:15 hr Z2 (@ 55 min, insert 15 min Z4)	40 min Z1 to Z2 (@ 10 min, insert PU)
Fri	60 min Z2 XT	60 min Z2 XT	60 min Z2 XT	60 min Z2 XT	45 min Z2 XT	20 min Z1, easy (in a.m.)
Sat	1:45 hr Z1 to Z2	2:15 hr Z1 to Z2	1:45 hr Z1 to Z2	2:15 hr Z1 to Z2	1:15 hr Z1 to Z2	Half Marathon!

Sun	Rest Day/Slide Day	Rest Day/Slide Day	Rest Day/Slide Day	Rest Day/Slide Day	Rest Day/Slide Day	Rest Day/Slide Day
Total	2:00–3:00 hrs XT 4:00 hrs Run 6:00–7:00 hrs Total	2:00–3:00 hr XT 4:30 hrs Run 6:30–7:30 hrs Total	2:00–3:00 hrs XT 4:15 hrs Run 6:15–7:15 hrs Total	2:00–3:00 hrs XT 4:45 hrs Run 6:45–7:45 hrs Total	1:45–2:30 hrs XT 3:45 hrs Run 5:30–6:15 hrs Total	2:30 hrs + Race

» *Training Program CC: Bare Bones*

Training Program CC: Bare Bones is for either the experienced half marathoner or the first-timer who is in good health, but due to either past injury history or future preventative reasons would prefer to base their half marathon preparation in cross-training (e.g., elliptical, pool running, cross-country ski, etc.) with only a minimal amount of actual running.

This program includes the two types of higher-intensity run sessions (i.e., Higher-Intensity Repeats and Higher-Intensity Inserts), plus the Long Run, but only one of the higher-intensity sessions is a run-only workout each week. The other Higher-Intensity Repeat session is completed using a cross-training option, and the Long Run is split between 50 percent running and 50 percent cross-training. In addition to these three sessions, there are two other moderate aerobic cross-training days.

There are also two Rest Day/Slide Days, one of which can be used as an optional moderate aerobic cross-training day, up to 60 minutes, at the athlete's option.

Program CC is best suited for athletes who fit Level Four in the Free Miles Training Hierarchy presented in Chapter 3. Tips on how to further customize this program to fit your individual needs are presented in Chapter 5.

Since the Z4 repeats in the Tuesday Higher-Intensity Repeat sessions will be completed using one of the cross-training options, they will be strictly based on heart rate and timed intervals. The higher-intensity portions will always be in Z3 to Z4, and the moderate portions will always be in Z1 to Z2.

For all Z4 portions in the Thursday Higher-Intensity Insert sessions, your target pace should be your 5K equivalent pace for all efforts of less than 8 minutes and your 10K pace for all efforts greater than 8 minutes in duration. Easily determine these paces using the chart in Chapter 4. Simply use your target half marathon time and pace to identify the equivalent 5K and 10K paces. Your Long Runs should be at 45 to 75 seconds slower than your Target Half Marathon Pace.

The longest of the Long Runs in this program peak at 2:15 hours.

HALF MARATHON TRAINING PROGRAM CC: BARE BONES

DAY/WEEK	Week 1 Sessions	Week 2 Sessions	Week 3 Sessions	Week 4 Sessions	Week 5 Sessions	Week 6 Sessions
Mon	30 min Z1 to Z2 XT	30 min Z2 XT	30 min Z2 XT	45 min Z2 XT	45 min Z2 XT	45 min Z2 XT
Tues	45 min Z1 to Z2 XT	45 min Z1 to Z2 XT	45 min Z1 to Z2 XT	60 min Z1 to Z2 XT (@ 10 min, insert PU)	60 min Z1 to Z2 XT (@ 10 min, insert 8 x 2 min Z4 @ 1 min easy)	60 min Z1 to Z2 XT (@ 10 min, insert 7 x 3 min Z4 @ 1.5 min easy)
Wed	Rest Day/Slide Day	Rest Day/Slide Day	Rest Day/Slide Day	Rest Day/Slide Day	Rest Day/Slide Day	Rest Day/Slide Day
Thur	45 min Z1 to Z2 run	45 min Z2 run	45 min Z2 run	45 min Z2 run (@ 30 min, insert PU)	60 min Z2 run (@ 45 min, insert 5 min Z4)	60 min Z2 run (@ 45 min, insert 7.5 min Z4)
Fri	30 min Z1 to Z2 XT	30 min Z1 to Z2 XT	30 min Z1 to Z2 XT	45 min Z1 to Z2 XT	45 min Z1 to Z2 XT	45 min Z1 to Z2 XT
Sat	30 min Z1 to Z2 XT + 30 min Z1 to Z2 run	37.5 min Z1 to Z2 XT + 37.5 min Z1 to Z2 run	45 min Z1 to Z2 XT + 45 min Z1 to Z2 run	52.5 min Z1 to Z2 XT + 52.5 min Z1 to Z2 run	60 min Z1 to Z2 XT + 60 min Z1 to Z2 run	67.5 min Z1 to Z2 XT + 67.5 min Z1 to Z2 run
Sun	Rest Day/Slide Day	Rest Day/Slide Day	Rest Day/Slide Day	Rest Day/Slide Day	Rest Day/Slide Day	Rest Day/Slide Day
Total	2:15 hrs XT 1:15 hrs Run 3:30 hrs Total	2:22.5 hrs XT 1:22.5 hrs Run 3:45 hrs Total	2:30 hrs Xt 1:30 hrs Run 4:00 hrs Total	3:22.5 hrs XT 1:37.5 hrs Run 5:00 hrs Total	3:30 hrs XT 2:00 hrs Run 5:30 hrs Total	3:37.5 hrs XT 2:07.5 hrs Run 5:45 hrs Total

DAY/WEEK	Week 7 Sessions	Week 8 Sessions	Week 9 Sessions	Week 10 Sessions	Week 11 Sessions	Week 12 Sessions
Mon	45 min Z1 to Z2 XT	45 min Z1 to Z2 XT	45 min Z1 to Z2 XT	45 min Z1 to Z2 XT	45 min Z1 to Z2 XT	45 min Z1 to Z2 XT
Tues	60 min Z1 to Z2 XT (@ 10 min, insert 5 x 4.5 min Z4 @ 2 min easy)	60 min Z1 to Z2 XT (@ 10 min, insert 4 x 6 min Z4 @ 3 min easy)	1:15 hr Z2 XT (@ 10 min, insert 3 x 7.5 min Z4 @ 3.5 min easy)	1:15 hr Z2 XT (@ 10 min, insert 10 x 3 min Z4 @ 1.5 min easy)	1:15 hr Z2 XT (@10 min, insert 5 x 6 min Z4 @ 3 min easy)	45 min Z1 to Z2 XT (@ 10 min, insert PU)
Wed	Rest Day/Slide Day	Rest Day/Slide Day	Rest Day/Slide Day	Rest Day/Slide Day	Rest Day/Slide Day	Rest Day/Slide Day
Thur	60 min Z2 run (@ 45 min, insert 10 min Z4)	60 min Z2 run (@ 40 min, insert 12.5 min Z4)	1:15 hr Z2 run (@ 55 min, insert 15 min Z4)	1:15 hr Z2 run (@ 55 min, insert 15 min Z4)	1:15 hr Z2 run (@55 min, insert 15 min Z4)	40 min Z1 to Z2 run (@ 10 min, insert PU)

Fri	45 min Z1 to Z2 XT	45 min Z1 to Z2 XT	45 min Z1 to Z2 XT	45 min Z1 to Z2 XT	45 min Z1 to Z2 XT	20 min Z1, easy (in a.m.)
Sat	52.5 min Z1 to Z2 XT + 52.5 min Z1 to Z2 run	67.5 min Z1 to Z2 XT + 67.5 min Z1 to Z2 run	52.5 min Z1 to Z2 XT + 52.5 min Z1 to Z2 run	67.5 min Z1 to Z2 XT + 67.5 min Z1 to Z2 run	37.5 min Z1 to Z2 XT + 37.5 min Z1 to Z2 run	Half Marathon!
Sun	Rest Day/Slide Day	Rest Day/Slide Day	Rest Day/Slide Day	Rest Day/Slide Day	Rest Day/Slide Day	Rest Day/Slide Day
Total	3:22.5 hrs XT 1:52.5 hrs Run 5:15 hrs Total	3:37.5 hrs XT 2:07.5 hrs Run 5:45 hrs Total	3:37.5 hrs XT 2:07.5 hrs Run 5:45 hrs Total	3:52.5 hrs XT 2:22.5 hrs Run 6:15 hrs Total	3:22.5 hrs XT 1:52.5 hrs Run 5:15 hrs Total	2:30 hrs + Race

INTEGRATING THE HALF MARATHON PROGRAMS WITH THE FULL MARATHON PROGRAMS

Can the half marathon programs be integrated with the full marathon programs? Yes. Should they be? Probably not.

In the full marathon programs in this book, the half marathon is used as a preparation race, not as an "A race." In other words, it is used as part of the preparation for a full marathon, which is the "A race." As you can see in the above three half marathon programs, if you are training for the half marathon as your "A race," you actually train differently for it.

So what does the athlete need to do who wants to make both "A races"? They simply need to spread out more. You could do the twelve- and sixteen-week programs back-to-back. Complete the twelve-week half marathon program and then, after racing the half marathon, transition right into the sixteen week full marathon program. However, this brings the entire training phase up to twenty-eight weeks. This is fine, but it can be accomplished faster while still truly training for both the half and full marathons as "A races." To do this, we suggest completing the half marathon plan and then transitioning right into week 7 of the full marathon program. The full length of this "double A race" approach will be twenty-two weeks, or about five months. By approaching it this way, we will train for both as true "A races" and can realistically expect to maximize our performances in both.

We hope the above training programs and tips help you to achieve your half marathon goals!

» NICK KING:
40-Plus Athlete Success Story

Nick King is an artist who lives with his family in Brooklyn, New York.

Nick took up road racing after turning forty and found that he had a lot of talent for it. Even with the basic type of "do a lot of mileage" training, he was able to record some impressive times. The problem he faced, however, was the same one that many over-forty athletes experience. Every time he was able to put some consistent training weeks together, he would become injured.

As many athletes do, Nick first came to us injured, frustrated, and looking for help with his training. He had first considered working out with the local running club. They had a weekly higher-intensity track session, but his gut feeling was that while that may be good for some twenty-something athletes, regular track training like that would just get him injured. He was probably correct.

We changed Nick's training approach; instead of focusing on lots of mileage, we embraced the Three Magic Bullets approach. We also talked about introducing more cross-training options to replace Nick's other sessions in addition to the Three Magic Bullets. Nick embraced this approach and suggested a great one to us: the ElliptiGO!

The ElliptiGO can be described as a combination between an elliptical machine and a bicycle. You propel it forward with an elliptical-type motion while standing. Not only is it a great running substitute that is done outdoors, but it is a lot of fun too.

With the combination of the Three Magic Bullets approach and the ElliptiGO cross-training, Nick enjoyed tremendous success. In his first full marathon with us, the New York City Marathon, Nick lowered his personal record by a full 5 minutes. A few months later in the Brooklyn Half Marathon, Nick set a substantial new personal record at that distance at well.

With Nick's natural talent, his embracing of the training approaches in this book, and his own cross-training creativity, he will surely be running many more fast marathons.

Fuel and Hydrate Like You Mean It

> *You cannot propel yourself forward by patting yourself on the back.*
> **—STEVE PREFONTAINE**

We are often surprised at the number of marathoners who greatly undervalue the importance of fueling and hydration, both in training and racing. For many, fueling and hydration are pretty much an afterthought done only when they feel hungry or thirsty.

To say the least, this is not a winning strategy. Getting the most from training means fueling and hydrating properly throughout the process and especially on race day. If an athlete waits until she feels hungry or thirsty, she has already waited too long.

This chapter will explain exactly how to fuel and hydrate before, during, and after all training sessions, and more importantly, before, during, and after races of all distances. This is especially important for the forty-plus athlete, who needs to ensure consistently high energy levels. A proper fueling and hydration plan will allow you to feel strong and energized when you need to be, to maximize training efforts and racing results.

THE IMPORTANCE OF PROPER FUELING

Stated simply, our bodies' two main fuel sources for the marathon are stored fat and glycogen (stored carbohydrate). While even the leanest athlete can store several times the amount of fat needed to run a marathon, the vast majority of athletes cannot store enough carbohydrates in the form of glycogen to maintain high energy levels for an entire marathon.

What happens when you run out of stored carbohydrates during a marathon? The phenomenon is known as the dreaded "bonk." The bonk is that horrible feeling you get when you run out of energy and it's all you can do to shuffle and jog to the finish line. Your body struggles because while it has enough fat fuel to keep moving forward, it is missing the other essential fuel—glycogen. Many jokingly describe the bonk as feeling like you are trying to run while carrying a piano on your back.

While most athletes use roughly 100 calories to run a mile, even the most highly trained athlete can only store about 2,000 calories in the form of glycogen. The actual amount varies from athlete to athlete, but that is pretty accurate for most runners. Simple math indicates that we only have the ability to store enough glycogen to get us through about 20 miles. Not surprisingly, if an athlete does not fuel properly during the marathon, the 20-mile mark is usually about the time when the bonk sets in. This is where the old marathon saying—"The second half of the marathon begins at 20 miles"—comes from.

Athletes have experimented with many "carbo-loading" strategies over the years to try to maximize glycogen stores prior to a marathon. Some of these strategies tend to be a little extreme. A popular approach years ago was to run a long run a week before the marathon, then consume almost no carbohydrates for three days. In the final three days before the marathon, the athlete would consume a diet highly concentrated in carbohydrates.

The idea was to trick your body into storing more carbohydrates than normally is possible. The shortcomings of this strategy were numerous. Not only was the additional amount of carbohydrates being stored very minimal, but the long run a week before the marathon had a negative impact on the athlete's taper, and the drastic shift from no carbohydrates to all carbohydrates often weakened the athlete's immune system.

The risks outweigh the benefits for most athletes. We prefer to approach it as "topping off glycogen stores," as opposed to "carbo-loading." Later in this chapter we will discuss strategies to top off glycogen stores as much as possible in the days leading up to your marathon.

Nuta Olaru, Masters Marathon champion

101 Degrees West

While you should make every effort to top off glycogen levels prior to your marathon, the important thing to know is that no matter how well you max out your glycogen stores, it is almost never going to be enough. You will always have to do more fueling during the race to ensure you have the energy to maintain your pace to the finish line. So in addition to stepping up to the starting line well fueled and well hydrated, you need to have a plan to take in carbohydrate-rich calories during the race.

THE IMPORTANCE OF PROPER HYDRATION

Marathon training and racing is not only about carbohydrates and glycogen stores. We need fluids, too. If we allow our hydration level to decrease below what our bodies require, we become dehydrated. In its early stages, dehydration gradually makes your body less and less efficient and eventually unable to maintain your target pace. Ultimately, if unchecked, dehydration can seriously endanger your health.

In our own training and testing, we have observed what is often described as "cardiac drift." If we did not hydrate properly during a long run, then along with feelings of thirst we would also notice that we would gradually need to increase our heart rates (i.e., increase our level of effort) to be able to maintain the same pace. In other words, we needed to gradually work harder and harder just to maintain the same speed. The more dehydrated we became, the less efficiently our bodies seemed to work. In contrast, when doing the same type of long run but staying consistently hydrated, we did not need to increase our heart rate to maintain pace, and in some situations it even decreased a little as the run continued at the same pace.

This demonstrates the importance of hydration to achieve your marathon goal. To maintain your target pace at a relatively stable level of effort, you need to maintain proper hydration levels. If you don't, you will have to work harder and harder to maintain your target pace, and then eventually you will not be able to maintain it no matter how hard you work.

DESIGNING YOUR FUELING AND HYDRATION PLAN

To run your best marathon, you need to be well fueled and well hydrated from start to finish. You also need to develop an optimal fueling and hydration plan that is unique to you. That's right: We are all different when it comes to fueling and hydration needs. The same fueling and hydration strategy that works for one athlete does not necessarily work for another.

Let's consider the following fueling and hydration strategy example: Bobby Boston is an experienced marathoner who weighs 150 pounds, with a goal to run a 3-hour marathon. He has tested several options in training and has developed what he believes to be his optimal fueling and hydration plan.

Bobby's plan is to consume one energy gel (100 calories) every 40 minutes during the marathon, for a total of four energy gels over the course of the race. He also plans to consume 20 ounces (150 calories) of an energy drink per hour, for a total of 60 ounces of energy drink over the 3 hours. Bobby's plan will result in approximately 283 calories and 20 ounces of fluid per hour. For a 3-hour marathon, this equates to 850 calories and 60 fluid ounces.

>> Calorie and Fluid Calculations

- Calories from energy gel: 4 x energy gel = 400 calories

- Calories from energy drink: 60 ounces of energy drink = 450 calories

- Calories per hour: 850 calories / 3 hours = 283 calories/hour

- Total calories for marathon: 400 + 450 = 850 calories/marathon

This is a typical fueling and hydration plan. Not only does this approach give Bobby enough calories and fluids to maintain high energy levels and good efficiency throughout his marathon (based on his testing during training), but assuming he was well fueled and well hydrated before the race started, it should help him to achieve his goal. While the quantities and sources of fuel and hydration may differ from athlete to athlete, this type of general approach works well for most athletes.

FUELING AND HYDRATION LOGISTICS

A successful fueling and hydration plan is more than just identifying our calorie and fluid needs and the fueling and hydration sources we will use to satisfy those needs; it also involves logistics. It's not only about what we need and when we need it, but it's also about how we plan to get it when we need it.

Unlike in the Tour de France bicycle race, no one will be riding along next to us in a support vehicle handing us our fueling and hydration sources at just the right time and in just the right quantities. We need to plan all of this out in advance and work with the resources available to us, which can differ from race to race.

Assuming 60 ounces of an energy drink is the optimal amount of fluid for Bobby to consume during his marathon, how can he be sure he is drinking 20 ounces of fluids per hour evenly during his race? First he needs to find out how many aid stations there will be in his marathon and, based on that number, practice drinking the proper amounts at each aid station to satisfy his plan. Typically the aid stations are evenly spaced out, but if not, it helps to know this and account for it in your plan.

In addition to knowing how many aid stations there will be in your particular marathon, you need to know exactly what fuel and hydration sources will be offered. Will some aid stations only offer water? What brand of energy drink and energy gel will be available? What other fueling sources might be offered—energy bars, bananas, etc.? This is all important information to consider when designing your plan.

In our example, Bobby wants to consume 60 ounces of fluid during the marathon. He finds out in advance of the race that twelve aid stations will be positioned roughly every 2 miles on the course. Based on this, Bobby calculates that he wants to consume about 5 ounces per aid station (60 ounces / 12 aid stations = 5 ounces per aid station).

The best way to prepare for hydrating during a race is to practice using cups in your training from time to time. Not only will you learn to drink efficiently from a cup while on the run, but you will also get to know what this amount (5 ounces) looks and feels like. This type of practice session can easily be accomplished on a track or a treadmill and can be included as part of one of your Long Runs or other regular training sessions. Put cups on a table next to the track and practice taking them at the proper time as you run laps around the track, or set them up on a table next to the treadmill. (Tip: Practice pinching the top of the cup as you drink to reduce spillage.)

Now how can Bobby be sure he gets his energy gels at the proper time during the marathon? Some athletes take gels (if available) from the aid stations, but we prefer to carry our own. There can be a lot of confusion at the aid stations when multiple runners come through at the same time, and you may get delayed trying to get exactly what you want. A well-intentioned volunteer may hand you the wrong item, or perhaps drop it. Energy gels are easy to carry, and if you carry your own, you can be sure to get the exact flavor you want and have it exactly when you want it.

In the above example, since the target marathon time is 3 hours, only four energy gels are required once the race starts (at 40 minutes, 1:20, 2:00, and 2:40), and that amount can easily fit into the back pocket of a running singlet. Practice running with the gel packets in your singlet so that you get used to the feel, or use a fuel belt and carry your gels in a flask.

To summarize our example: Bobby Boston first tested his fueling and hydration sources and quantities in training and determined his optimal plan. Then he developed the logistical side of his plan based on the aid station setup for the specific marathon he was planning to do. When he stepped up to the starting line, he had the confidence of knowing he had a complete fueling and hydration plan. He knew exactly what he was going to consume and exactly when he was going to consume it.

DETERMINING YOUR HYDRATION NEEDS

So how can you determine your optimal fueling and hydration plan? Let's start with determining your hydration needs. The athlete in the above example targeted 20 ounces of fluid per hour. How can you know what amount is best for you? Our suggestion is to use a sweat-rate test to determine your hydration requirements. There are various approaches to this, but our simple approach is the following:

» Sweat-Rate Test

- Weigh yourself (unclothed) just prior to beginning your run
- Run for 60 minutes in Z2 (75–85 percent of maximum heart rate) while not consuming any food or fluids and not urinating
- Weigh yourself (unclothed) immediately after the run
- Complete the following calculation: Weight Before – Weight After = Hourly Sweat Loss
- Record the air temperature at the time of the test

Following is an example demonstrating how to use the sweat-rate test and how to interpret the results:

- Weight Before = 165.0 pounds
- Weight After = 163.75 pounds
- Sweat Rate = 165.0 – 163.75 = 1.25 pounds = 20 ounces

In this example, the athlete will require about 20 ounces of fluid per hour to maintain his fluid levels.

As a next step, we suggest repeating this test in different heat conditions. This is important because we sweat more or less at various temperatures. If we can use the above formula to determine what our sweat rate is at 50, 60, 70, or 80 degrees, then we will know how to adjust our fluid intake on race day based on the weather conditions. Finally, we suggest repeating the test in workouts that include higher-intensity levels (e.g., Z3 and Z4) because sweat rate may change slightly due to intensity level.

DETERMINING YOUR CALORIE SOURCES

Determining your hydration needs is the key first step. From there you can determine the type of energy drink, the type of energy gel, or perhaps other fueling sources you want to use. We prefer energy gels for their simplicity, effectiveness, and ease of carrying. Most marathoners feel the same, although some prefer energy bars, bananas, or other fuel sources. These are all fine as long as you thoroughly and frequently test each of the sources you plan to use during training to make sure they work well for you. Also, plan and practice all of the logistics for the sources you plan to use.

Different brands of energy drinks and energy gels differ from one another, with different ingredients and different calorie totals. Some contain caffeine and some do not. We personally prefer GU Hydration as our energy drink and GU energy gels, but experiment to find what works best for you.

If you plan to get any of your fuel sources at the aid stations, then you should know exactly where the aid stations will be on the course and exactly what items will be available. If, on the other hand, you plan to carry everything you need, you should know exactly how you plan to do so, and practice it regularly in training.

Finally, you should determine how many calories per hour you need to target. In the Bobby Boston example, we had a 150-pound athlete who determined through testing during training that approximately 283 calories per hour worked best for him. Test this out yourself in training as you determine your optimal calories.

Find the calorie level that makes you feel the best. It will vary from athlete to athlete depending on size and other factors. Most marathoners fall within the range of 200 to 400 calories per hour. Too many calories per hour may make you feel bloated. Too few calories per hour may make you feel low on energy. Ultimately you want to determine the optimal level of calories and overall plan that makes you feel highly energized without feeling bloated or uncomfortable.

FUELING AND HYDRATION ARE TRAINABLE

Here is a little secret that the majority of runners don't know: Our ability to become comfortable using various types of fueling and hydration sources and certain quantities of fueling and hydration is trainable. That's right! Even if a particular fueling source or quantity doesn't appeal to you on your first try, it doesn't mean you should not practice with it more and see if you can become accustomed to it.

We often see athletes using a certain type of energy drink while they train, only to discover when they get to the race that that particular hydration source will not be offered on the course. They use the source that is offered, it doesn't agree with them, and their performance suffers. This is really a rookie mistake. You should check the race website prior to the race and find out exactly what will be provided. If it's something you don't usually use, you should consider getting some and training with it. Like we said, our ability to become comfortable with a certain type of hydration source is trainable. Get some, use it in training, and be prepared to use it on race day.

There are other options, such as carrying your own hydration source in a fuel belt, but this greatly complicates your race and should be a fallback position.

Likewise, what if once you complete the sweat-rate test you find that you should be consuming more than you currently do? Our suggestion is not to ignore it. Instead, start to work toward that amount in training. Increase gradually and allow your body an opportunity to get used to the greater quantities.

When should you practice fueling and hydration in training? As far as fluid replacement goes, always. You should try to take in your needed fluid replacement in all your training sessions. If your requirement is 20 ounces per hour, that's what you should try to do consistently in training.

As for fueling, however, we suggest practicing it only on longer workouts of 90 minutes or more, and not for shorter sessions. If you begin the workout fully fueled and hydrated, on shorter runs you don't really need all of those calories (and you definitely don't need the expense of energy gels and energy drinks). Our simple guideline is the following:

- For training runs up to 90 minutes, hydrate just with water at the rate determined by your sweat-rate test.

- For training runs of 90 minutes or more, hydrate with an energy drink and fuel with energy gels just as you plan to during your marathon. In other words, practice your exact fueling and hydration race plan.

Additional tip: When practicing your fueling and hydration race plan in your longer training sessions, occasionally skip the fueling part for the last 30 to 45 minutes of the run. Keep hydrating with water, but stop taking in calories in the form of gels and energy drinks. If timed well, this will bring on a slight bonk at the very end of your run, which is a great training opportunity both for your mind and body. We don't recommend doing this regularly, but once or twice a month will help you to prepare mentally and physically to conquer the bonk should it happen in your marathon.

PRE-RACE FUELING AND HYDRATION

We are often surprised to see athletes work so hard for several months to prepare for their marathon, only to blow it by poor fueling and hydration leading up to the race. As mentioned earlier, there are a lot of complicated carbo-loading schemes out there, but we find they cannot take the place of good common sense. In general, it doesn't make sense to make any changes, especially to your diet, right before a major race.

We find athletes do best when they have a smart, balanced year-round approach to healthy eating (see Chapter 9, "Leaner Is Faster") and continue this right up until the last forty-eight to seventy-two hours before the marathon. Then, over the last forty-eight to seventy-two hours, we suggest you skew your diet toward carbohydrates. Not any new or different types of foods, just the same foods you usually eat, with a greater mix of carbs. Some of Don's favorite carbohydrates are the usual foods—pastas, rice, breads, and energy bars—but he also likes to snack on pretzels over the last two or three days before the race. This helps to top off his glycogen stores, as well as his sodium stores.

You should also hydrate well over the last forty-eight to seventy-two hours. This doesn't mean gulping down bottles of water. Instead, keep an energy drink with you over the last two days and gradually sip it. If your urine stays clear and light, it probably means that your hydration levels are pretty good.

Water is good, but combining water with an energy drink is better. Water alone can dilute your sodium levels if you take in too much. If you stick with an energy drink over the last two or three days and combine it with the types of foods we discussed, you will go to bed the night before your race with both your glycogen and sodium levels topped off nicely.

RACE MORNING FUELING AND HYDRATION

The morning of the race is the most important time for properly fueling and hydrating your body. We typically suggest waking at least three hours before your marathon and eating right away. This should be a carbohydrate-rich and easily digestible meal. Popular foods for this are toast with jelly, bagels, muffins, waffles, oatmeal, or cereal. It is important that you test your pre-race meal several times in training and make sure it works for you. The morning of the race is no time for experimentation.

Coffee or tea and water are fine to drink with your pre-race meal, but then it's best to switch over to an energy drink. The pre-race energy drink we prefer is GU Hydration, which is the same one we use in training.

Each athlete is different, and you should test in training to determine what works best for you. The following is an example of a simple and effective pre-race routine for one particular elite age-group athlete we coach:

- Wake up at least three hours before the race and consume two energy bars, 12 ounces of bottled water, and 8 ounces of coffee.

- Over the next 2.5 hours until start time, gradually sip two 20-ounce bottles of an energy drink.

- Consume one GU energy gel with a couple of ounces of water 10 minutes before the race start.

Now let's do the math on this pre-race fueling and hydration routine for this successful 150-pound athlete:

Total Calories Consumed

400 = Two energy bars
300 = Two bottles of energy drink
100 = One GU energy gel
800 = Total pre-race calories

Total Fluid Consumed

12 ounces of bottled water
8 ounces of coffee
40 ounces of energy drink
60 total pre-race ounces of fluid

Most athletes tend to consume less than the 800 calories and 60 ounces of fluid that this elite age-group athlete does in the three hours leading up to his marathon. As mentioned earlier, all athletes are different, and what works for one will not necessarily work for another. But in general we find that most athletes do not consume enough calories and fluids before a race and that their performances usually improve with increases to their pre race fueling and hydration plan. So consider these levels and use the tools in this chapter to help you determine the best plan for you.

Most importantly, keep testing, practicing, and perfecting your pre-race and race fueling and hydration plan as part of your weekly training. Then once you get within a couple of weeks of your race, end the experimentation and stick with the plan you have developed and practiced during your sixteen-week marathon training cycle.

POST-RACE AND POST-TRAINING FUELING AND HYDRATION

There is a window of opportunity of approximately forty-five minutes after races and training sessions to really jump-start your recovery and prepare your body for the next day's training session. If you miss this window, your glycogen levels do not replenish as quickly as they are capable of doing, and your body may not get the nutrients it needs to repair itself in a timely manner.

For best results, try to consume 200 to 350 calories of combined carbohydrates and protein within this forty-five-minute window after all races and training sessions. This will jump-start the restoration of your glycogen stores and help your body to repair damaged micro-muscle fibers. You will recover faster and be much better prepared for the next day's training.

There are several recovery drinks available on the market. We personally prefer Pro Series Muscle Milk, which includes about 7 grams of carbohydrates and 32 grams of protein. Other foods we like to use for this purpose are low-fat yogurt or energy bars with a greater balance of all three nutrients: proteins, fats, and carbohydrates.

We hope this discussion will help you to develop your optimal fueling and hydration plan. We also hope that if you hadn't already appreciated the importance of fueling and hydration, you do now. Fueling and hydration should never be an afterthought. It's a key element to our marathon success. So let's be sure to fuel and hydrate like we mean it!

» SORIN CIOCAN:
40-Plus Athlete Success Story

Sorin Ciocan is an executive in the international supply chain business who currently lives with his family in Hong Kong.

Sorin came to us for coaching after reading the first edition of this book. He had recently run his best time so far at the Paris Marathon, but then soon after found himself injured again. This time it was a stress fracture, but he had previously experienced many of the other common running injuries as well. Sorin was approaching marathon training like many other marathoners do, and it seemed to have brought him to a point of plateauing performances and injury. He wanted to take a new approach to his training and see if he could improve his results and stay healthier.

One of the challenges Sorin faced was that because of his career he did a lot of traveling, which made training consistency a challenge. Not only would there be time zone changes and busy days to deal with, but he would also be challenged by inadequate training facilities and a lack of proper places to run.

In addition to his traveling challenges, he has also had to move his home a few times due to his career. Each time he moved, it created challenges and interruptions to his training. Most recently he has moved to Hong Kong, which, like any very large city, has its training challenges for sure.

We changed Sorin's training approach; instead of focusing on mileage and other traditional elements, we embraced the Three Magic Bullets approach. We also talked about introducing more cross-training options to replace Sorin's other sessions besides the Three Magic Bullets. Despite all this, the Three Magic Bullets approach to training has served him well. Since working with us he quickly set a new personal record in the half marathon, and then followed that up with a new personal record in the full marathon. In fact, since working with us he has recorded four marathon performances faster than his old personal record.

Next on his list of goals is to complete the Boston Marathon, which he will be aggressively pursuing this year. Now that he is healthy and more injury-free, Sorin also plans to take on ultra-distance challenges in the future, the first of which will be the Courchevel X Trail 54-kilometer run. Watch for Sorin as he continues to build his performances and run faster and faster marathons after forty.

» Core and Functional Strength Training, Dynamic Warm-up, and Stretching

If you want something you've never had, you must be willing to do something you've never done. **—THOMAS JEFFERSON**

The road is paved with good intentions when it comes to core and strength training, dynamic warm-up, and stretching. Although there is plenty of evidence out there to support the benefits, we still often neglect to incorporate all or some of these into our running regimen. For most of us, it is the time element; we just don't have enough time. For others, strength training can be intimidating and not something we particularly enjoy. When our running season begins, we ditch the strength training for extra mileage on the road. And who has time for a dynamic warm-up before running or a proper stretching routine after finishing the run . . . right?

The reality is, core and strength training go hand in hand with marathon training or any distance running. It can help in a few different ways: 1) by improving overall muscle imbalances that cause injuries, especially as your running volume increases, 2) by building those muscles that enable you to maintain good form and running efficiency even as you fatigue, and 3) by improving your ability to run faster and longer.

A good time to incorporate strength training, dynamic warm-up, and stretching was probably ten years ago, but the next best time is now. No matter where you are in the cycle of your training, there are exercises you can do to help improve your running efficiency and form and avoid injury.

It is widely known that as we age, we begin to lose muscle mass, flexibility, and range of motion in our joints. There are many reasons for the aging process to take hold. That is why it is important to sometimes forgo quantity over quality and maintain these three elements in your training at some level. In the off-season it is best to increase your core and strength training and work on those muscle weaknesses and imbalances, while during the racing season, it is best to pare it back and do more stretching and functional training.

If you have to shorten your run by five minutes to do a proper dynamic warm-up, it will be well worth it. We all dislike that feeling of the first ten or twenty minutes of our run, when we feel stiff and tight. The dynamic warm-up will help minimize that feeling by warming up your muscles, elevating your core body temperature, and preparing your body to begin your workout. It will help to stave off injuries and have you feeling ready for a run. This is true of a post-run stretching routine as well. In as little as ten minutes, we can help our muscles to recover from our run and prepare us for the next day's workout.

Let's start with the dynamic warm-up that we do and that we recommend to our athletes. It can take as little as five minutes but will prepare your body for the workout that lies ahead. After sitting for hours at a desk or doing a manual-labor job, the body is often not prepared to endure the pounding of a high-intensity or long run.

DYNAMIC WARM-UP: THE NIFTY NINE

1. PRESS-UPS

Begin by lying flat on the floor, facedown, with your hands close to your armpits and under your shoulders. Take a deep breath and then, as you exhale, begin lifting your torso off the floor while straightening your arms but keeping your hips on the floor. Keep your buttocks relaxed and let your belly fall to the floor. Repeat this movement ten times.

2. CHILD'S POSE

From the starting position of the press-up, sit back on your bent knees so your buttocks are touching your feet. Keep your arms stretched out about shoulder-width apart in front of you with your head down. Hold that position for a count of 30 seconds.

3. HAMSTRING AND CALF RAISES

From child's pose, keeping your head down and your arms straight, raise your buttocks toward the ceiling, straightening your legs. Then, while keeping one leg straight, bring your other leg behind it and place your foot so it rests on the heel of your straight leg. Keeping your head down, start with the foot flat on the floor, rise up onto your toes, and then lower the heel back down to the floor. Repeat this movement ten times before switching legs and repeating the movement ten more times.

4. WINDMILLS TO HI-LO PROPELLERS

Start in a standing position with good posture and your arms at your sides. Raise one arm straight up above your shoulder and then bring it back down and repeat with your other arm, all in a fluid motion for a total of twenty times. Then bring your arms straight out from your sides, starting from a high position and gradually lowering your arms to your sides as you swing them around your body in a propeller fashion, allowing your hands to relax and your elbows to bend around your body. Repeat this movement for five rotations lowering your arms down, and then five more rotations to swing your arms back up again.

5. FRONT TO BACK KICKS

Start in a standing position with good posture and holding onto something stable with one hand. Begin by swinging one leg in a kicking motion forward and then backward, repeating this movement ten times. Then turn so your other hand is holding onto something stable and repeat this movement with the other leg ten times.

6. SIDE STEP/SQUAT

Start in a standing position with feet together. Take a step to your right with your right leg, then squat back and touch your fingers to the floor between your legs. Then return to a standing position, bringing your left leg to your right leg, and repeat the movement ten times in that same direction. Then, step with your left leg in the opposite direction and repeat the movement ten times in that direction.

7. ACROSS-BODY LEG SWINGS

Start in a standing position holding onto something stable in front of you. Swing your right leg across your body in front of your left leg and then swing it back to the right. Repeat this movement ten times. Then switch legs and repeat this movement with your left leg ten times.

8. REVERSE CROSS LUNGE WITH KNEE HUG

Start in a standing position with your feet shoulder-width apart. Lunge back with your left leg, bringing it behind your right leg and to the side (to about 7 or 8 o'clock) and touch the top of your right foot with your left hand. Flex your knee back to a straight leg, bring your left knee up to your chest, and grab hold of it with both hands for a three-second count. Repeat that movement ten times. Then repeat the movement ten times while lunging back with your right leg.

9. RUN HOP/SKIPS

Start in a standing position with your feet together. Begin by hopping on one leg while simultaneously raising the other leg with bent knee and touching that knee with both hands out in front, and then repeating with the other leg in a skipping motion. Repeat the movement twenty times, alternating legs while maintaining good posture and keeping hips aligned.

It may take you a few times to get efficient at doing these dynamic exercises, which for some may be more like a workout, but once you do, you'll find your body craves this type of a warm-up every time you run. And you will realize these five minutes are well worth it.

So you finished your run; you grab something to drink and are ready to get home to be with your family. It sounds like a good idea, and hydrating is a good idea; however, if you want to wake up the next morning without a lot of soreness and stiffness, it's best to take five minutes and do some basic stretching.

Here are eight post-run stretches that will help you to recover and prepare for your next workout. If you practice these stretches daily, you can complete them in a matter of five minutes if you are pressed for time. However, if you have extra time, extend these stretches by holding them for longer periods.

STRETCHING EXERCISES: THE AWESOME EIGHT

1. DOWNWARD DOG STRETCH

The downward dog is a basic yoga stretch. Start by standing with feet wider than shoulder-width apart. Reach out with both hands toward the floor in front of you while extending your pelvis toward the ceiling. Gradually press your heels into the floor as you straighten your arms and legs. Relax your back as you hold this pose for a count of 30 to 90 seconds.

2. HIP FLEXOR AND PSOAS STRETCH

From a standing position, take one step forward into a lunge position with both knees bent and the back knee on the floor. Raise the arm on the opposite side of the forward leg, straight up toward the ceiling, and lean slightly forward, stretching the psoas muscle. Hold this position for 30 seconds. Then bend that same arm slightly over your head to stretch your hip flexor for a count of 30 seconds. Repeat these two stretches with the opposite leg forward.

3. CHEST AND NECK STRETCH

Keeping your fingers together, interlock your hands behind your back and straighten your arms. Gently pull your hands down, depressing your shoulder blades as you stretch your chest and pectoral muscles for a count of 30 seconds. Then turn your head to the side toward your shoulder and hold for 5 to 10 seconds; repeat on the other side for a count of 5 to 10 seconds.

4. STANDING QUAD STRETCH

Start in a standing position with feet together. Bend the knee of one leg and raise your foot behind you. Reach behind you with the same or opposite hand, bringing the knee parallel to your other knee. Keep your back flat and hold for 30 seconds, then repeat with the other leg.

5. PIRIFORMIS AND GLUTE STRETCH

Start in a standing position, holding onto something stable if necessary. Cross one ankle over the other knee and push your hips back into a sitting position, holding the stretch for 30 seconds. Switch legs and repeat the stretch for 30 seconds.

6. GROIN STRETCH

Start by sitting on the floor with your legs outstretched in front of you. Bend both your knees, bringing the soles of your feet together with your hands. Gently press your knees toward the floor with your elbows and hold for 30 seconds.

7. CALF STRETCH

Start by standing on a step or stair with both feet. Then take one foot and bring your toes to the edge of step while dropping your heel toward the floor, and hold that stretch for 30 seconds. Switch feet and repeat the stretch for 30 seconds.

8. FOOT STRETCH

Start by standing in front of a wall or step. Bring one foot close to the step and raise your toes onto the wall or step while stepping back with the opposite leg. The back leg can be either straight or bent.

As we age, our muscles lose their suppleness, causing a shortened stride, which may lead to joint pain. By stretching after a run, you can mitigate some of those aches and pains you typically experience and keep your muscles loose and supple.

Can you find ten minutes in your workout to do both a dynamic warm-up and a solid stretching routine? Sure you can—cut your workout by ten minutes and sacrifice quantity over quality. You will find your body feels much better and you can fend off some very unnecessary injuries.

Now to the meat of the discussion: How do we build or keep our muscles strong as we age? Do we have to hire a personal trainer or join a CrossFit or strength class? For some this is the answer, but for those who would rather do it on their own, we have a plan that will help you. You can follow this plan at home with little equipment or at the gym.

We break our core and strength training program into three basic training cycles: "Off-Season," "Pre-Season," and "In-Season." In our off-season, we are running less mileage and therefore we have more time to do strength training. This season can last from one to four months or more. During our pre-season and in-season cycles, we may be ramping up our volume (time or distance and intensity) and want to avoid further breakdown of our muscles. Our pre-season exercises would last about one to two months, while our in-season program begins about four weeks out from our first race and continues until we take a break from racing.

You can tie these exercise segments to our sixteen-week marathon training programs found in Chapter 5 as follows:

Weeks 0–5: Off-Season Core and Strength Training*
Weeks 6–10: Pre-Season Plyometrics
Weeks 11–14: In-Season Maintenance Program
Weeks 15–16: No Core or Strength (use time to do extra stretching)

You can also tie these exercise segments to our twelve-week half marathon training programs found in Chapter 6 as follows:

Weeks 0–1: Off-Season Core and Strength Training*
Weeks 1–4: Pre-Season Plyometrics
Weeks 5–8: In-Season Maintenance Program
Weeks 9–12: No Core or Strength (use time to do extra stretching)

---

* The "Off-Season" can be done anytime you are not in a specific training program. So, anytime before you start the sixteen or twelve weeks and anytime after the sixteen or twelve weeks.

Read through the exercises and make sure you understand how they should be performed and are capable of doing so without causing pain or injury. Also confirm that you have all the equipment you will need.

SUGGESTED EQUIPMENT

- **Stability ball**—round inflated ball in various sizes to fit your height (e.g., 35 cm, 45 cm, 65 cm, 75 cm, etc.)

- **BOSU® ball** (acronym for "both sides utilized")—inflated ball with a flat side and a half-dome side, used to develop balance and stability on an uneven and unstable surface

- **Medicine ball**—round weighted ball with a rubberized coating available in various weights from one to fifteen or twenty pounds

- **Dumbbells**—weighted bars in various coatings such as plastic or metal, and weights from one pound to fifty-plus pounds

- **Resistance band**—a continuous loop band made of latex about 12 inches in diameter and about 1 to 3 inches wide; comes in varying resistances

- **Kettle bell**—a large cast-iron or plastic-coated bell-shaped weight with a flat bottom and rounded, thick handle at the top

- **Step**—an elevated platform made of plastic and adjustable with various risers to increase height

The goal of the Off-Season exercises is to begin with the basic exercise for a period of two to three weeks and then advance the program by doing the first and second progressions each for a period of two to three weeks. This will allow us to work on our stability and strength as we advance the exercises.

CORE AND STRENGTH TRAINING: OFF-SEASON

1. SQUATS WITH ARM RAISES

a. Start by standing with your feet about shoulder-width apart and turned slightly out. Begin by extending your butt back and bending your knees, bringing your quads about parallel or lower (if you can) to the floor. Simultaneously, raise your arms straight out in front of you so they are parallel to the floor as well. Three sets of 12 to 15 repetitions (reps).

b. Progression 1: With dumbbells—same as above, except point your toes forward, not outward, and hold a dumbbell in each hand at your sides the entire time. Form is the same otherwise. Three sets of 10 to 12 reps.

c. Progression 2: One-leg squat with dumbbells—same as above, except holding a dumbbell in each hand, raise one leg behind you or in front of you and perform the squat with only one leg. Three sets of 10 to 12 reps each leg.

2. SIDE LUNGE WITH DUMBBELL REACH

a. Stand with your feet together and holding a dumbbell in each hand. Take a large step to the left with your left leg, bending the knee and lunging while keeping your right leg relatively straight. Bring the left arm to the outside of the right leg, closer to your foot, and keep the right arm closer to the inside of your right leg. Then push off on your left foot to return to the start position. Three sets of 10 to 15 reps each leg.

b. Progression 1: With curl and press—same as above, except as you return to the start position, simultaneously curl the weights with your biceps and then extend your arms straight over your head into a shoulder press, alternating legs each time. Three sets of 10 to 12 reps total.

c. Progression 2: With curl and press—same as Progression 1, except perform a transverse lunge instead of a side lunge. Three sets of 10 to 12 reps total.

3. LEG CURLS WITH STABILITY BALL

a. Lie on your back on the floor with your legs straight and both feet on top of a stability ball and your arms straight at your sides. Begin the exercise by raising your torso and hips off the ground so that you form a straight line from your shoulders through your hips to your feet. Then pull your feet back toward your buttocks while maintaining that straight-line position. Return your legs to the straightened position and repeat the movement. Three sets of 12 to 15 reps.

b. Progression 1: Same as above, except after forming your bridge and pulling your feet back, raise one leg off the ball and then return to the start position before placing the raised leg back on the ball again. Three sets of 10 to 12 reps each leg.

c. Progression 2: Same as Progression 1, except after forming the bridge with both legs, raise one leg off the ball, pull back with the other foot, and then return to the start position while the leg remains off the ball for all of the repetitions. Three sets of 10 to 12 reps each leg.

4. FRONT LUNGE

a. Start by standing with feet together and a dumbbell in each hand. Begin the exercise by taking a step forward, keeping your back straight and bending your knee to bring your quadricep parallel to the ground. Then push off with the front foot and return to the start position, alternating legs each time. Three sets of 10 to 20 reps.

b. Progression 1: Same as above, except lunge onto a BOSU ball. Three sets of 10 to 20 reps.

c. Progression 2: Same as Progression 1, except hold a light weight in your right hand and a heavier weight in your left hand. Lunge forward onto the BOSU with your left leg and simultaneously raise your right arm in an arcing motion with your palm facing up over your head. Press off with your left foot and return to the start position, bringing your right arm back to your side. Repeat with the same leg for 10 to 12 reps before switching the weights and lunging with the opposite leg for 10 to 12 reps.

5. PULLOVERS OVER STABILITY BALL WITH MEDICINE BALL

a. Start by sitting on a stability ball, holding a medicine ball in both hands. To begin the exercise, roll out from the ball, bringing your shoulders, neck, and head onto the ball so your chin faces the ceiling while forming a bridge from your hips to your knees. Engage your abdominals and keep a straight line from your shoulders to your knees while raising the medicine ball straight up toward the ceiling. Begin the exercise by lowering the medicine ball over your head with your arms straight, without hyperextending your shoulders, and then engage your lats to pull the medicine ball straight up over your chest to the start position. Three sets of 12 to 15 reps.

b. Progression 1: Same as above, except perform the exercise with only one arm, using a lighter medicine ball and keeping the other arm at your side. Three sets of 10 to 12 reps each arm.

c. Progression 2: Same as basic exercise, except hold a dumbbell in each hand. Three sets of 10 to 15 reps

6. DUMBBELL ROWS ON ONE LEG

a. Start with feet together and a dumbbell in each hand. Bend at the hips, bringing your torso toward the floor and raising one leg behind you so it is parallel to the floor, while lowering the dumbbells with palms facing each other. Begin the exercise by raising the dumbbells in a rowing motion, pulling your elbows back but close to your sides. Keep your back flat and engage your abdominals. Switch legs halfway through the repetitions. Three sets of 12 to 15 reps.

b. Progression 1: Same as above, except hold a dumbbell in your left hand, raise your left leg off the ground, and then perform the rowing motion, completing all the repetitions before switching to the other hand and leg. Three sets of 10 to 15 reps each arm/leg.

c. Progression 2: Start by standing in a staggered position with your left foot forward while the right leg remains back and on the floor and a dumbbell in your right hand. Straighten your right arm toward the floor with knee bent, and then in a rhythmic motion pull the arm back and twist the torso while the opposite arm comes forward. Perform all repetitions on that side before switching to the opposite side. Three sets of 12 to 15 reps each side.

7. PUSHUPS WITH HANDS ON A STEP

a. In a facedown position, place your hands a little beyond shoulder-width apart on a step in front of you. Extend your elbows so that your body is in a neutral position. Begin the exercise by flexing your elbows and bringing your chest toward the step while maintaining a neutral spine. Then push up, extending your elbows back to the starting position. The higher the step, the easier the pushup. Three sets of 10 to 15 reps.

b. Progression 1: Same as above, except raise one leg off the floor and perform half the repetitions before switching legs and performing the other half of the repetitions. Three sets of 5 to 10 reps each leg.

c. Progression 2: Same as basic exercise, except perform the pushup with feet together on the floor. At the top of the pushup, rotate your torso while simultaneously raising your arm toward the ceiling and balance in a side plank. Then return the arm to the step and perform the next repetition while raising the opposite arm. Three sets of 10 to 15 repetitions.

8. FRONT PLANKS

a. Lie on the floor in a prone position with your elbows directly under your shoulders and your weight on your forearms. Raise your legs, hips, and torso, forming a straight line from your shoulders to your ankles, and hold. Avoid allowing your hips to sag. Three sets of 30 to 90 seconds.

b. Progression 1: Same as above, except perform one-leg raises while holding the plank position. Three sets of 5 to 10 raises each leg.

c. Progression 2: Same as Progression 1, except do the plank with your arms straight. Three sets of 5 to 10 raises each leg.

9. SIDE PLANKS

a. Lie on your side on the floor with your elbow under your shoulder and your legs straight and feet stacked on top of each other. Avoid allowing your hips to sag. Hold the position for 30 to 90 seconds each side.

b. Progression 1: Same as above, except do one-leg raises in the side-plank position. Three sets of 10 raises each leg.

c. Progression 2: Same as Progression 1, except do the plank with a straight arm. Three sets of 10 raises each leg.

10. REVERSE PLANK

a. Lie on the floor on your back with elbows bent under your shoulders and legs straight. Raise your buttocks and legs off the floor so your torso is parallel to the floor and your body is in a straight line. Avoid allowing your hips to sag. Hold the position for three sets of 30 to 90 seconds.

b. Progression 1: Same as above, except do one-leg raises with foot flexed (toe pointed toward shin) in the reverse-plank position. Three sets of 10 to 12 raises each leg.

c. Progression 2: Same as Progression 1, except keep your arms straight in the plank position while raising the leg. Three sets of 5 to 10 raises each leg.

PRE-SEASON PLYOMETRIC EXERCISES

These exercises are done primarily using just your body weight and are performed quickly and explosively. The intensity is high, so we bring down the sets and reps to reduce muscle wear and tear and allow recovery. This phase will help to prepare you to finish strong in your races.

1. ONE-LEG RAISE TO LUNGE

a. Start in a standing position with feet together. Raise one knee toward your chest and then kick out into a forward lunge, bending both knees. Alternate legs with every repetition. Perform these lunges in a quick and more explosive way without using any weights. Two to three sets of 10 reps.

2. HOPS

a. Start by standing with feet together and knees slightly bent. Hop forward with both feet, continuously and quickly, 5 to 10 times, and then backward 5 to 10 times. Two to three sets of 5 to 10 reps.

b. Progression 1: Side-to-side hops—same as above, except hop diagonally forward to one side and then diagonally forward to the other side for 10 hops forward, and then repeat backward. Two to three sets of 5 to 10 reps.

c. Progression 2: One-leg hops forward and backward or diagonally forward and backward. Two to three sets of 5 to 10 reps.

3. JUMP SQUATS

a. Start by standing with feet about shoulder-width apart and in a squat position and then jump, extending your legs straight up. Land in the squat position and repeat quickly. Two to three sets of 5 to 10 reps.

b. Progression 1: Same as above, except jump onto a step or bench. Two to three sets of 5 to 10 reps.

c. Progression 2: Same as Progression 1, except jump with one leg onto a step or bench. Two to three sets of 5 to 10 reps.

4. ONE-LEG SQUAT WITH FOOT ON STEP

a. Start by standing on a step with your left foot only and your right leg bent and off the step. Bend at your hips and flex your knee, bringing your right foot to the floor. Just touch with your toe and then extend back up again. Repeat with the other leg. Two to three sets of 5 to 10 reps each leg.

b. Progression 1: Same as above, except go right into a hop after extending back up. Two to three sets of 5 reps each leg.

5. SIDE STEP IN SQUAT POSITION

a. Start in a standing position with feet together. Begin by lowering into a squat position, hold that position, then take a step to the right with your right leg and bring your left leg to your right foot. Repeat for 10 repetitions in one direction and then return by taking a step with your left leg and repeating for 10 repetitions in the other direction. Two to three sets of 5 to 10 reps each direction.

b. Progression 1: Same as above, except with an ankle band around your ankles for more resistance. Two to three sets of 5 to 10 repetitions each way.

6. BURPEES

a. Start in a standing position, then begin the exercise by dropping into a squat position. Bring your hands to the floor, then kick both legs back into a plank position with arms straight. Jump your legs back to your hands to return to the squat position before standing up. Two to three sets of 5 to 10 reps.

b. Progression 1: Same as above, except when you get to the plank position, add a pushup before jumping back to the squat position and standing up. Two to three sets of 5 to 10 reps.

c. Progression 2: Same as Progression 1, except add a jump at the end after standing up. Two to three sets of 5 to 10 reps.

7. STRAIGHT-ARM PLANKS WITH ROTATION

a. Start by kneeling on all fours in front of a bench facing out. Raise one leg at a time, placing your toes on the bench until you are in plank position with arms straight. Keeping arms straight, bend one knee and bring it across your torso toward the opposite elbow. Then return the foot to the bench and repeat with the other leg. Two to three sets of 5 to 10 reps each leg.

b. Progression 1: Same as above, except before returning the leg to the bench, rotate your hips and bring your leg back and behind so you are stretching your hip and flexors, then bring your foot back to the step, alternating legs each time. Two to three sets of 5 to 10 reps each leg.

8. WINDSHIELD WIPER

a. Start by lying flat on your back with your arms out to the sides and feet together on the floor with knees bent. Raise your legs off the floor, keeping knees bent, and rotate your legs to the right side, just about touching the floor, and then return to the start position and repeat to the left side, keeping your shoulders and back on the floor. Two to three sets of 5 to 10 reps each side.

b. Progression 1: Same as above, except straighten your legs and rotate side to side. Two to three sets of 5 to 10 reps.

c. Progression 2: Same as Progression 1, except hold a barbell in your hands straight over your chest and bring your feet straight up and toward one end of the barbell, then back and toward the other end of the barbell. Two to three sets of 5 to 10 reps.

IN-SEASON MAINTENANCE EXERCISES

These exercises are meant to help us maintain our strength while keeping the weights light and bringing down the intensity. With fewer exercises in the maintenance phase, this opens up opportunities to do more things like stretching, foam roller work, and self-myofascial release.

1. CURTSY LUNGE WITH BICEP CURL

a. Start in a standing position with your feet together and a dumbbell in each hand. Raise one leg and bring it behind, bending both knees, and across the other leg while simultaneously performing a bicep curl. Return to the start position and alternate legs on each repetition. Two to three sets of 10 to 12 reps.

b. Progression 1: Same as above, but begin by standing on a step or elevated platform. Alternate legs on each repetition. Two to three sets of 10 to 12 reps.

2. ONE-LEG DEADLIFTS WITH KETTLE BELL

a. Start in a standing position with your feet together, holding a kettle bell in both hands. Lower your body by bending at your hips, reaching one leg behind you while lowering the kettle bell toward the floor. Keep the standing knee slightly bent and maintain a flat back throughout the exercise. Two to three sets of 10 to 15 reps each leg.

b. Progression 1: Same as above, except hold the kettle bell in your left hand while extending the left leg back. Then repeat the same number of repetitions with the kettle bell in the right hand while the right leg extends back. Two to three sets of 10 reps each leg.

c. Progression 2: Same as Progression 1, except when you return to the standing position, raise the kettle bell up and over your head in a shoulder-press position. Two to three sets of 10 to 12 reps each leg/arm.

3. BOX STEP UP AND LOWER

a. Start in a standing position parallel to a box or step. Begin the exercise by raising the closest leg onto the step while bringing the other leg off the floor. Then slowly lower that leg to the floor. Take the other foot off the step and repeat this motion for the full number of repetitions before switching legs. Two to three sets of 10 to 15 reps each leg.

4. ROW IN PLANK POSITION

a. Start in a kneeling position on the floor with a dumbbell in one hand. Reach out into a prone position, keeping both arms straight, with hands directly in line with your shoulders and your body in a straight line. Begin by raising the dumbbell in a rowing position, keeping your back flat, and then return to the floor. Repeat for the total number of repetitions before switching arms. Two to three sets of 10 to 15 reps each arm.

b. Progression 1: Same as above, except with a dumbbell in each hand. Begin by raising one dumbbell in a rowing position, keeping your back flat, and then return to the floor. Repeat with the opposite arm and then alternate arms each time. Two to three sets of 10 to 15 reps each arm.

5. PUSHUPS WITH CLAP

a. Start with your hands on an elevated bench or platform, keeping your legs straight and body in alignment. Lower your chest to the bench or platform, then press up with enough force to clap your hands before you return to the bench or platform. Two to three sets of 10 to 15 reps.

6. RUSSIAN TWISTS WITH MEDICINE BALL

a. Start by sitting on the floor with your legs together in front of you, knees bent, and a medicine ball at your side. Begin by grabbing hold of the medicine ball with both hands and simultaneously raising your feet off the floor, leaning slightly back. Bring the medicine ball across your body to the other side, allowing your torso to twist and the medicine ball to touch the floor but not rest on it. Then swing the medicine ball back to the starting point. Two to three sets of 10 to 15 reps.

There are certain things we can do to combat the aging process and improve performance, from our daily nutrition to exercise. But what also has been shown to improve the quality of life as we age is a core and strength training program, a dynamic warm-up, and a consistent stretching program that keeps muscles loose, supple, and working and functioning properly so you remain physically strong. It will not only help you to achieve your running goals but also help with the everyday tasks of living and enjoying life.

Take some time and review this chapter so you can train and race to your potential. Find what works best for you, incorporate it into your running regimen, and stick with it. The benefits are endless and there is no better time to start than now.

» Leaner Is Faster

Many of life's failures are people who did not realize how close they were to success when they gave up. —STEVE PREFONTAINE

One of the running truths that most athletes hate to accept is that leaner is faster. If all else is equal, we are generally fastest at our leanest healthy body weight. Many athletes train hard and assume that either they will get as lean as they need to be as a result of training alone or their body will naturally seek its own unique optimal weight through the training process. Unfortunately this is not true. We achieve our optimal and fastest lean body weight through a combination of effective training and proper nutrition.

The clearest proof of this is in the measurement of VO2 max. This is a popular test that determines an athlete's ability to process oxygen and convert it to energy. It is the most common assessment of endurance capacity, and universities and health clubs across the country offer the test for a small fee. Not surprisingly, world-class marathoners record the highest results for VO2 max.

The easiest way an athlete can improve his results in a VO2 max test is by losing weight. That's right, if all other variables are equal, your VO2 max results will improve with a simple decrease in body weight. Logically this makes sense: If the engine stays the same but you lighten the load, the vehicle becomes faster. It's a simple matter of the power-to-weight ratio.

Knowing this, it's no surprise that the vast majority of world-class endurance athletes have body weights well below average. Undoubtedly, an athlete can take this to an extreme and get so thin that he or she becomes unhealthy and weak by losing muscle mass. There will always be some people who, for whatever reason, take a good thing too far. But generally our lightest healthy weight is usually our fastest weight.

This focus is especially important for the forty-plus athlete. As we get older, it becomes more and more challenging for most athletes to maintain their weight. Many experience a gradual creep in weight gain as they age. Does this mean that you are not going to achieve your goals unless you lose twenty pounds? Absolutely not. But one of the ways we will get there is by achieving a lean, healthy body. This chapter will present the exact step-by-step process for athletes to follow to get their body weight to where it needs to be to achieve their marathon goals. Of course we will not only look to lighten the load, but also to increase the power of the engine.

There are many benefits to eating smart and achieving a lean, healthy body weight. We have personally discovered that by eating healthily, training properly, and achieving our optimal race weight, not only do we perform better athletically, but also our cholesterol, blood pressure, and other vital signs are better than ever. Though never the specific goal, those added bonuses are certainly a welcome side effect. For all of us forty-plus athletes, this is very important.

Because we feel strongly that athletes should strive to be healthy and achieve a natural balance in all areas of life, we are not big fans of the various diets out there. They seem to be primarily short-term in focus, and at some point the dieter returns to his same old ways and his same old weight—or even heavier. One possible exception might be the Weight Watchers program, because it teaches individuals to eat real food in proper portions and in real-life situations. Some endurance athletes are successful with the Weight Watchers approach.

For anyone who is committed to being healthy and fit for life, the optimal path is to find the proper balance of nutrition and training that will allow you to be the athlete and the healthy person you were meant to be.

Before starting any diet or nutrition plan, we encourage you to seek the advice of a competent nutrition expert. Let us say right up front that we are not nutrition experts. What we talk about in this chapter is based on personal experience with our own training and nutrition and the feedback we have received from the hundreds of athletes we have worked with over the past decades. So consider what we have to say, but before starting your own plan, get guidance from a certified professional.

Aya Stevens, elite runner and professional triathlete
James Mitchell Photography

SIX SMALL MEALS

The key to our success, and that of many of our coached athletes hoping to get leaner and achieve optimal race weight, was a switch to eating six small meals every day. That's right. Get away from the traditional "three square meals a day" approach and start eating more frequently. Rather than eating three big meals averaging 800 to 1,200 calories each (plus additional snacking in between), try to consume six smaller meals, averaging 400 to 600 calories each.

Over the years we have observed many positives to this approach. An athlete's energy level is steadier throughout the day because the calories are being distributed gradually over a longer period of time. Instead of high and low energy swings, an athlete's energy level is more constant and consistent.

This approach felt natural to us immediately, and it continues to feel that way today. Our coached athletes have reported the same experience. They are constantly on the go all day long. In addition to their training, they have career and family responsibilities. With the six-meals-a-day approach, these athletes experience high levels of energy, both physical and mental, when they need it during the day. Another benefit of this approach is that you rarely get that "full" feeling after eating and thus can fit in your run at any time of the day.

How do we arrange the six small meals? Let's look at them as three mini meals and three big snacks. Here's an example of how it might work for a particular athlete:

5:00 a.m. Wake up and early morning snack
5:30–6:30 a.m. Run training session
7:30 a.m. Mini breakfast
10:00 a.m. Mid-morning snack
12:30 p.m. Mini lunch
3:30 p.m. Mid-afternoon snack
4:30–5:30 p.m. Core and functional strength workout
6:30 p.m. Mini dinner
10:00 p.m. Bedtime

Note the spacing of the meals; typically they are two to three hours apart. Spreading them out evenly helps to keep your energy level more constant throughout the day. Note also that we have already consumed four of the six meals by midday, effectively "front loading" our calories a bit toward the beginning of the day. This makes perfect sense because our physical and mental needs are at their highest then. It mirrors the old adage: Eat breakfast like a king, lunch like a prince, and dinner like a pauper.

Consistent with this approach, the last of the six meals is at 6:30 p.m.; we do not eat again until the following day. This makes good sense, too. There is no need to take in a lot of calories before bedtime when we don't need them. Late-night snacks are likely to be stored as fat. One possible exception to this is if you do an evening workout. It may then be helpful to have a light, healthy snack after your evening workout.

With a 10:00 p.m. bedtime, this may mean up to three hours without eating after dinner. This is one of the most challenging time periods of weight management. It's so easy to have a late snack that will put you over on calories for the day. If you find it helps to hold you over, a small snack of 100 calories or fewer between dinner and bedtime is fine, but be careful not to allow this to lead to a late-night calorie binge.

If you find evening snacking to be a challenge, consider drinking water or hot decaffeinated tea after dinner to help suppress your appetite. Another strategy is to brush your teeth right after dinner. Brushing our teeth sort of tells us we are done eating for the day.

There are many fans of the six-meals-a-day approach, and several versions of it out there. Most agree on the same benefits of this approach. On the website FitFAQ.com, editor Jamie Clark lists the following benefits:

More energy
Less hunger
Reduced food cravings
Control blood sugar and insulin production
Reduce body fat storage
Maintain and increase lean muscle mass

We have personally experienced these same benefits, and many of the athletes we work with report the same findings.

DO I NEED TO COUNT CALORIES?

Counting calories certainly helps! Each person's body has a certain unique number of calories it needs to maintain its current weight. To sort of state the obvious, if we consume less than this amount over time, we tend to lose weight. If we consume more than this amount over time, we tend to gain weight.

Through years of trial and error, Melanie has determined that 1,500 calories per day seems to be the amount that maintains her 125-pound body weight, net of training. In other words, if she did no training and just performed normal daily activities, her weight would remain fairly constant if she consumed 1,500 calories per day.

Furthermore she has found, through trial and error, that if she eats about 500 fewer calories per day (1,500 – 500 = 1,000 calories), she tends to lose weight at a rate of about one pound per week. Likewise, if she eats about 500 calories more than this amount per day (1,500 + 500 = 2,000 calories), she tends to gain weight at the same rate of about one pound per week.

If you can determine what your unique calorie maintenance number is, you can have a great deal of control over your weight. Put yourself in the position of being able to adjust your weight over time by adjusting your daily calorie intake. The technical term for this is basal metabolic rate (BMR). In layman's terms, this is the amount of energy your body uses just to keep it functioning. While Melanie originally determined her unique BMR through trial and error, there are many websites that can help you to estimate yours, and this may be a good place to start.

Let's say you had your best racing year ever last season, and you were competing at a body weight of 175 pounds. With this year's racing season only two months away, you find you've gained some weight over the winter and are now weighing in at 183 pounds. You want to safely reduce to your "race weight." No problem. If you know your calorie needs as per the example above, you can make that simple 500-calorie adjustment each day, and you will gradually lose about one pound a week. In only eight weeks you should be down around your "race weight."

Why do we want to lose weight gradually as opposed to losing it quickly? Our personal experience has been that if you lose the weight very gradually, you are far more likely to keep it off. What's more, often when individuals lose weight rapidly, they feel weak, and some even report a higher risk of illness as a result. Finally, rapid weight loss tends to take the good with the bad. We are far more likely to lose our good lean muscle as well as our unwanted excess fat. So always play it safe. If you want to lose weight, do it gradually and safely and under the supervision of a qualified professional.

IS IT OKAY TO EAT OUT AT RESTAURANTS?

Eating out is fine, but unless you are very disciplined and have a thorough knowledge of exactly how many calories are in most types of foods, it's best to eat out in moderation. The reality is that if we eat out at a restaurant more than a couple of times a week, it is almost impossible to know how many calories we are consuming. There are usually so many hidden calories in restaurant food. Our suggestion is to limit yourself to restaurants no more than two times per week and to try your best to make good food choices when you do.

If you find yourself eating out more often, consider the following tips:

- Limit or eliminate your consumption of alcohol. Hydrate well before and during your meal with water with lemon or lime.

- Start your meal with a salad with light oil and vinegar, as opposed to a high-calorie salad dressing.

- Order simple main dishes without a lot of mystery ingredients (which translate to hidden calories).

- Avoid sauces, especially those made with cream, butter, or other high-calorie ingredients.

- Avoid fried foods in favor of grilled or baked foods.

IS IT NECESSARY TO BE THIS ORGANIZED WITH YOUR NUTRITION?

Although not essential to running a faster marathon, if you are serious about maximizing your performance, we encourage you to embrace a serious approach to your eating habits and nutrition.

Athletes often tell us they are discouraged because their weight is not where they would like it to be. When we ask them what they are doing to become leaner, they often tell us they are "trying to lose weight." We have learned that this is just a buzz phrase. What it really means is that they are hoping to lose weight from training alone and "watching what they eat," but they are not really focusing on how much they are actually eating—that is, their specific calorie intake.

When we ask these athletes how many calories they are consuming, they may throw out a number, but with a little probing we usually find that they really don't have any idea. With a little more probing, we often find that they consume many hidden calories throughout the day that they don't remember. We jokingly refer to this as "snack amnesia."

Snack amnesia situations lurk around every corner. It was someone's birthday in the office, so they had a piece of cake. They spent several hours tailgating before the football game. They went out to a big dinner with a client. They went out for drinks and snacks after work with coworkers. It's easy to lose track of your calorie intake in situations like these. Chances are that unless you are really focused on your calorie intake, scenarios like this will keep popping up during the week, and you will be regularly taking in a lot more calories than you think you are. Remember: An average of just 500 extra calories per day can mean one pound of weight gain per week.

One of our favorite excuses is, "I have children so I have to have cookies and ice cream around the house." Of course this is not true. Why would we want to teach our children that ice cream and cookies should be part of a normal diet? We will discuss the concept of "reward foods" later in this chapter.

Because it's so easy to fall into snack amnesia, we encourage you to dial in on exactly how many calories you consume and exactly how many you burn during training.

WHAT ABOUT CALORIES BURNED WHILE TRAINING?

This all sounds easy enough to figure out, but what the weight maintenance example does not take into account is calories used in training. This complicates the calculation a bit, and this is where most athletes go off track.

If we need to consume a specific number of calories per day to maintain our weight, net of training, how much do we need to consume *with* training? This becomes even more complicated when we consider that we do different types of training on different days, with varying durations and intensity levels. It is not as if each day we use the same amount of calories.

For example: In Melanie's case, if she needs 1,500 calories per day to maintain her body weight, and she uses an average of 800 calories per day in training, then she would need to consume 2,300 calories per day (1,500 + 800 = 2,300 calories) to maintain her weight and some amount less than that to lose weight. Since Melanie does different activities every day, she has developed a range of calories for all of her various sports activities, and she estimates her calories based on the duration of the activity and her perception of the intensity of the workout.

Following are the calorie ranges that she finds work best for her:

Core and strength training: 200 to 400 calories per hour
Elliptical/cross-training: 400 to 600 calories per hour
Run training: 600 to 800 calories per hour

For example: If Melanie did a low-intensity one-hour run session in the morning and then had a moderate one-hour core and strength session in the late afternoon, she might assign 600 calories for the run session and 300 calories for the core and strength session. This means that she would apply a combined negative 900 calories (600 + 300 = 900 calories) to her calorie totals for the day, to compensate for her training activity. If her estimates are correct, and her needed calorie consumption to maintain her weight is a net 1,500, then to maintain her same weight, she would try to consume about 2,400 calories that day (1,500 + 900 = 2,400 calories).

This approach has worked well for Melanie over the years. She keeps track of the calories she consumes and those expended in her various sports activities, and as a result she has developed a good feel for what her calorie and training needs are in order to get her weight to where she wants it to be, to be healthy and race her best. But, just like determining your own unique calorie needs, you need to determine calorie ranges for the training activities you participate in. It takes a little work, but we suggest this approach to any athlete trying to achieve a healthy, lean race weight.

There are many resources available to help you estimate your own calorie ranges for your activities. Two good websites to consider are myfitnesspal.com and loseit.com.

BALANCED CALORIES

Not all calories sources are the same. Carbohydrates, proteins, and fats each do different things and all play a role in a healthy diet. While we often hear about "protein diets," "low-fat diets," and many other trendy approaches, we have found that a well-balanced healthy diet and proper portion control have usually worked best for us as athletes.

What does the US Department of Agriculture (USDA) consider to be a healthy diet? Its Dietary Guidelines for Americans describe a healthy diet as one that:

- Emphasizes fruits, vegetables, whole grains, and fat free or low fat milk and milk products

- Includes lean meats, poultry, fish, beans, eggs, and nuts

- Is low in saturated fats, trans fats, cholesterol, salt (sodium), and added sugars.

None of these points should surprise anyone. After years of trial and error, we find these guidelines fit right in with the optimal approach to eating for us and for many of our coached athletes, which includes healthy carbohydrates, proteins, and fats. Only when we are getting all three of these, in the right ratios, do we feel our best and perform at our best as athletes.

Many experts say a diet of 40 percent carbohydrates, 30 percent protein, and 30 percent fat works best for most people. While Don's best ratio is a little different (more like 50 percent carbohydrates, 25 percent protein, and 25 percent fat), we have found that most athletes we work with are fairly close to these suggested ranges. So if you are looking for a good place to start, we suggest beginning with the popular 40-30-30 ratio.

In a recent *Runner's World* magazine, Ryan Hall, a top American marathoner, says, "I never have a problem consuming enough calories, one reason why I think I am a good marathoner. But I make sure each meal or snack has protein, healthy fats, and carbohydrates."

While we find that maintaining our ratio on a daily basis keeps our energy level at its highest, we feel even better still when each of our six small meals includes the same ratio as well. It's almost impossible and probably not worth the effort to calculate the exact ratio for every meal, but we find that if we can at least include all three calorie sources in each meal, with the goal of hitting our ratio for the entire day, we can remain at the absolute most consistent level of energy throughout the day.

HYDRATION

This one is big! Hydration is so important, and we see too many athletes not giving it the attention it deserves. We all know how critically important proper hydration levels are to athletic performance, but for some reason hydration only becomes a focus around race time. Hydration needs to be a part of your diet every day. It will keep you feeling well and ready to get the most from every training session. Even a modest 2 percent dehydration occurring prior to or during exercise can negatively impact performance.

When an athlete tells us he is feeling a little blah, the first thing we ask him about is what his hydration has been like recently. We often find that his fluid intake has not been what it should be. We make a correction, and it's amazing how often it improves his energy level.

Now if we are feeling a little blah, the first thing we do is grab a nice cool bottle of water from the refrigerator. Next to sleep, it's one of the best things we can do to get the most from our training. In fact, most times when an athlete tells us she is feeling a little fatigued and rundown, we suggest she take the day off, get some extra sleep, and get fully hydrated.

One other great benefit of maintaining proper hydration levels is that most people find if they are well hydrated, they feel less hungry. This can be very helpful if you want to keep cravings under control, as dehydration can often cause a sensation of hunger.

REWARD FOODS

Needless to say, there are certain foods that really aren't that good for us and should not be part of our regular diet. We all have certain foods that are hard to stay away from, despite the fact we know we should. Here's how we deal with this, as do many of our coached athletes. Instead of cutting these foods from your diet completely, designate them as "reward foods." In other words, instead of deciding you can never have these foods again—a promise you know you cannot keep—decide to treat yourself to them only as a reward for certain accomplishments.

For Don, it's french fries—the saltier the better. He doesn't want french fries to be part of his regular diet, but doubts he can say good-bye to them forever. So french fries are one of his primary reward foods.

After a good race, he will usually have french fries as part of his post-race celebration. Sometimes he even hits the drive-through window on the way home. This approach keeps them in their proper place in his overall diet, and he enjoys them even more when he eats them because it feels like an extra celebration.

We often joke with our athletes about our "twenty-four-hour rule." This means that after a good marathon they are allowed to eat "reward foods" for the next twenty-four hours. While we mean it half-jokingly, an interesting benefit usually occurs with this approach. After eating glazed doughnuts for twenty-four hours straight after a big race, the athlete gets pretty sick of them and is more than happy to get back into training and wait until after the next big race to eat them again.

HEALTHY EATING EXAMPLE

When we talk to our coached athletes about nutrition, they often ask, "Can you just give me an example of what you eat?" While we understand that this is a tempting approach because it is a lot simpler than devising a plan from scratch, it's important to remember that the optimal diet for any athlete is unique to that person. That's why we suggest working with a professional to determine what is best for you. But to give an example of how to approach this, the following would be a typical day for Melanie based on the following requirements:

Targeted net calories of 1,500
Estimated range for calories burned during specific workouts:
Core and strength training: 200 to 400 calories per hour
Elliptical/cross-training: 400 to 600 calories per hour
Run training: 600 to 800 calories per hour

Target ratio of 40 percent carbohydrates, 30 percent protein, and 30 percent fat

5:00 a.m. Wake Up and Early Morning Snack (400 Calories)
Coffee with skim milk
Energy drink
Energy bar
GU energy gel
Water

5:30–6:30 a.m. Run Session (Net Negative 450 Calories)
Lower-intensity run = 600 calories
Consumed energy drink = 150 calories

8:00 a.m. Mini Breakfast [300 Calories]

Oatmeal with walnuts and raisins
Low-fat Greek yogurt with fruit
Water

10:30 a.m. Mid-Morning Snack [300 Calories]

Apple slices with almond butter
Cottage cheese with pineapple
Water

12:30 p.m. Mini Lunch [400 Calories]

Salad with grilled chicken, feta cheese, peppers, carrots, and almonds with olive oil and balsamic vinegar
Rice cakes
Water

3:30 p.m. Mid- to Late Afternoon Snack [200 Calories]

String cheese
Apple slices
Whole-grain wheat flatbread
Water

5:00–6:00 p.m. Core and Strength Session [Net Negative 150 Calories]

Moderate-intensity core and strength session = 300 calories
Consumed energy drink = 150 calories

6:30 p.m. Mini Dinner [500 Calories]

Grilled chicken mixed with whole-wheat pasta, olive oil, tomato sauce, sun-dried tomatoes, mozzarella cheese, broccoli, and onions
Steamed brussels sprouts with olive oil
Slice of Italian bread
Water

10:00 p.m. Bedtime

Calculations
2,400 calories consumed
900 calories utilized in training
1,500 net calories

RESOURCES

We hope you find our comments on healthy eating to be helpful. As we said in the beginning of the chapter, consider our suggestions but before taking action, consult a nutrition expert. Always be safe and proceed with caution.

Following is a list of a few of the resources available to help you with your nutrition planning:

www.usda.gov
www.foodsafety.gov
www.weightwatchers.com
www.myfitnesspal.com
www.loseit.com

➤➤ STEPHEN GROSSMAN:
40-Plus Athlete Success Story

Stephen Grossman is an insurance executive who lives with his family in suburban New Jersey.

While he had been a high school tennis player and track team member many years ago, Stephen decided he wanted to get back into competitive athletics the year he turned forty. He came to us for help in achieving his goals. One of the most important was to complete his first marathon at the 2009 New York City Marathon and eventually qualify for Boston.

We introduced Stephen to our marathon training approach, and it suited him very well. In fact, his consistent success and steady improvement over the past several years has been extraordinary.

Stephen accomplished his first marathon in New York with a very respectable first marathon time of 3:50. Stephen loved the training and enjoyed being back in competition, so he went right to work on improving his marathon fitness and times. To say he was successful would be an understatement.

At the 2010 New York City Marathon he lowered his time an amazing 28 minutes to 3:22. But Stephen was not stopping there. A year later at the Atlantic City Marathon he brought it down to 3:06 and qualified for the Boston Marathon. And then in 2013 at the Monster Mash marathon, he went under 3 hours for the first time with a 2:58. In a period of just three years, Stephen went from a very respectable time to a truly elite time for an over-forty athlete and has qualified for the Boston Marathon many times over.

Sadly, Stephen's wonderful string of successes was brought to a pause when he suffered a terrible bike crash while training and sustained many serious injuries. He has been recovering over the past several months, and we are happy to report that he has finally been able to run again. There is no doubt that Stephen's persistence, drive, and commitment to proper training will have him back running elite-level marathons in the very near future. Watch for Stephen running many more fast marathons after forty.

» Secrets to Staying Injury-Free

I plan to be running as long as I can and have no plans to stop. —FRANK SHORTER

Running injuries are so common we often like to joke with our coached athletes that the human body was not built for running. In fact, injuries are the number one reason athletes don't achieve their goals and the number one reason they stop running altogether.

This is especially true for more mature athletes. The older we get, the greater the risk of injury and the greater the likelihood of giving up running entirely. The trick is to avoid injury or at least minimize the downtime due to injury.

The most common reason for injury is what many athletes refer to as "overtraining." It can more accurately be described as "too much too soon."

The human body can successfully become stronger if training volume is increased at the proper rate. This is called the "principle of gradual adaptation." The mistake many athletes make is they don't progress gradually enough. Impatiently, they take big jumps forward in their training, before their bodies have fully acclimated to the last increase. This leads to breakdown, not adaptation.

This chapter will present powerful strategies both for avoiding injury in the first place and what to do when you do get injured (which we hope is very rare) to quickly return to good health. Athletes who tend to take a proactive and preventative posture against injury are usually injured less frequently and for less time. But what steps should a marathoner take to develop this type of proactive and preventative posture?

The following is our five-point injury prevention and reduction strategy:

1. Proper Running Technique
2. Running and Racing Shoe Selection
3. Effective Warm-up and Cooldown
4. Core and Functional Strength Training, Dynamic Warm-up, and Stretching
5. Early Detection and Timely Follow-up of Common Running Injuries

PROPER RUNNING TECHNIQUE

There are many differing opinions on proper running technique, and we encourage you to keep an open mind when considering the best approach for you. Most importantly, run tall. Your upper body greatly influences your lower body. The most common mistake we see among runners is leaning too far forward in the direction they are running. Stand up straight and erect. Hold your chin up and look straight ahead. Allow your shoulders to roll back slightly. Swing your arms forward and backward, not side to side. Relax your face, shoulders, and hands. The approach that we have found works the best and helps to keep most athletes less prone to injury is the "Two Strings" Approach.

≫ "Two Strings" Approach

While running, visualize one string attached to the very top of your head and gently pulling you upward. As you picture this in your mind, allow yourself to "run tall" in an upright position and allow your shoulders to drop and relax. Many athletes describe this as visualizing yourself as a marionette.

Next visualize a second string attached to the middle of your chest and gently pulling you straight forward in the direction you are running. As you visualize this, allow your shoulders to roll back slightly in a chest-first position. Your arms should swing relaxed in a forward-and-back motion, not a side-to-side motion.

That is all there is to the "Two Strings" position. What this position does is align the top half of your body so that the bottom half is free to run naturally without having to compensate for improper balance in the torso. With proper alignment and balance, our legs and feet tend to follow their natural range of motion. No side-to-side motion here either. Keep everything moving in a straight line, front and back.

We have personally used this technique for over twenty years, and after all this time we still do the visualization on each and every run—once at the start, when we want to get our run off to a good beginning technically; a second time, usually at the heart of the workout; and then once more, toward the end, to make sure that our technique is not slipping when we are most tired.

Give the "Two Strings" Approach a try and see how it makes you feel. If you are like most runners, we think you will find it to be helpful.

» Additional Tips

- Avoid bouncing or loping while you run. This is a common mistake. The energy you exert pushing up against gravity is wasted. You want to glide along close to the surface and only exert the minimal amount of energy necessary to resist gravity. To correct this technique flaw, try looking at a stationary object off in the distance. As you stare at the object, it should remain steady. If you find that it is bouncing in your view, begin reducing the upward push in your running gait, until the bouncing stops. To train yourself to always run smoothly, repeat this exercise several times on each run.

- Consider having a gait analysis done by a competent professional. There are many sports trainers, podiatrists, chiropractors, and physical therapists with excellent training and abilities in gait analysis.

» Hill Running

Hill running is a technical area of running that can certainly cause injury if not done properly.

Ascending: Many athletes try to take large, bounding steps up a hill, which is inefficient and can cause injury. We find the best way to approach hills is to lean forward slightly, shorten your stride a bit, and increase your leg turnover. By using this approach, you will stay closer to the surface and spend less energy battling gravity.

Descending: Descending is also very important. Many runners try to take long, gliding steps, as if they want to try to take greater advantage of gravity. But this energy is wasted, and the runner often loses control of his running and struggles just to maintain balance. This wild flailing down the hill is dangerous because it puts excessive stress on the leg joints. This is of particular concern for the forty-plus athlete who is typically more prone to injury. As is the case with ascending, when descending it is best to shorten your stride, increase your leg turnover, and run in an efficient and controlled manner.

RUNNING AND RACING SHOE SELECTION

Another important step in the prevention of injuries is to have the optimal running shoes for your specific biomechanics and physiology. All runners are unique, and the best shoes for one athlete are not necessarily the best for another. We suggest visiting a good running store and having a competent professional suggest the best shoe for you based on the way you run, your training volume, and your injury history.

EFFECTIVE WARM-UP AND COOLDOWN

The wise forty-plus athlete knows that he cannot "jump-start" and "crash-stop" his body in training every day year after year and expect to remain injury-free. All marathoners, but especially those over forty, need to ease into running with a proper warm-up and end with a proper cooldown.

When muscles are properly warmed up before being worked out hard, they are far more injury-resistant. The approach we find that works best for over-forty athletes is to start all runs with a walk of five to ten minutes in addition to the dynamic warm-up presented in Chapter 8. Start slowly and gradually build to a brisker pace. Then, when you feel ready, begin to run. Resist the temptation to immediately jump into the heart-rate range suggested in the workout. If the workout suggests Z2, for example, allow yourself five minutes to gradually work up into it.

Likewise, don't stop abruptly at the end of your training session. Allow your heart rate to come down gradually and the activity of your muscles to gradually ease. Bring your speed down over the last few minutes of your run and then immediately transition into a walk. A five- to ten-minute walk at the end of your run will allow your body to safely transition from the run and into a post-workout recovery.

Chapter 4's discussion on training races also presents specific suggested warm-up and cooldown approaches for racing that can be incorporated along with the above approach. Also, in Chapter 8 on strength training, you can find a suggested post-run stretching routine.

CORE AND FUNCTIONAL STRENGTH TRAINING, DYNAMIC WARM-UP, AND STRETCHING

Core and functional training, dynamic warm-up, and stretching are not activities to focus on only when you are injured. Part of taking a proactive preventative posture toward injury is to build core and functional strength training, dynamic warm-up, and stretching into your regular weekly training. Nothing will help you to become more injury-resistant than to build functional and balanced strength and increase your range of motion.

Chapter 8, "Core and Functional Strength Training, Dynamic Warm-up, and Stretching," explains our strength program, dynamic warm-up, and post-run stretching exercises.

EARLY DETECTION AND TIMELY FOLLOW-UP OF COMMON RUNNING INJURIES

Fine-tuning your running technique, finding the optimal running shoes, incorporating a warm-up and cooldown in your training, and building proper strength training, dynamic warm-up, and proper post-run stretching into your program all will go a long way toward preventing and reducing injury, but you also need to be focused on the early warning signs of injury and be prepared to take action if necessary. A key element in accomplishing this is "listening" closely to your body for these early warning signs.

Many old-school athletes subscribe to a "no pain, no gain" philosophy and try to ignore the early warning signs of injury. Don used to be much the same way. He was more inclined to see pain as "the enemy," and would either ignore it or try to push through it. He believed his perseverance would win out over the pain. Of course, this is a flawed strategy and usually leads to small injuries becoming big injuries.

He no longer views pain signals as the enemy. He sees them as early warning signs that can help him head off minor issues before they grow into major ones. If anything, pain signals are helpful in guiding us to do the right thing to ensure our long-term good health.

We believe all serious athletes should frequently consult with qualified medical professionals, beginning with a thorough annual physical. As part of the physical, make the doctor fully aware of your training program and request his or her feedback on it.

From there, you should consider assembling a full team of medical specialists available to you if the need arises. Having been competitive endurance athletes for over thirty-five years, our team includes a general practitioner, chiropractor/ART® specialist, podiatrist, orthopedist, and a physical therapist. We don't see any of them regularly, except of course for the annual physical, but when any need arises, we go quickly to the expert on our team who we feel can best help. By taking a proactive stance on injuries and having a ready team of specialists to consult, we find that we are able to jump on any issue early and head it off before it becomes a problem.

One of the keys to long-term marathon success is staying healthy. And the best way to stay healthy is to be very proactive with injuries in terms of early detection and treatment. So consider our suggested five-point injury prevention and reduction strategy. Examine each point and compare it to what you are currently doing. Identify the areas in which you can become more proactive and consistent.

Always put your health first. You want to be a successful marathoner, but you want to be an athlete for life, too. Listen closely to your body, treat any aches and pains seriously, and get frequent consultations with competent medical professionals.

»DAVE MANTLE:
40-Plus Athlete Success Story

Dr. David Mantle is a dentist who lives with his family in London.

Before coming to us for coaching, Dave had been a marathoner for many years and had completed several marathons with a pre-forty personal-record time of 3:10.

Having recently turned forty and feeling that his improvement may have stagnated, Dave came to us for coaching help. Dave was looking to us to help him take his marathon performance to a new level and possibly even break the 3-hour mark.

We of course introduced Dave to our Three Magic Bullets approach to marathon training, and he soon began to see his times improving. In his first marathon with us, and his first marathon after turning forty, he recorded a new personal-record time of 3:08. It was a good start, but it was just that, a start. In his next marathon, Dave further lowered his personal record to 3:05. Around that same time, Dave was also lowering all of his personal records for the major standard racing distances of 5K, 10K, and the half marathon. Any fears of stagnation were now gone; Dave's performances were on the move.

The big breakthrough came a year later when Dave recorded an amazing time of 2:57 at the Valencia Marathon. He didn't just achieve his sub-3-hour goal, but sprinted right by it. In an e-mail sent moments after the race, Dave wrote, "I could cry I'm that happy. Just bagged that elusive sub 3 in 2:57:31!!!!! How good is that, I'm so over the moon! When I started marathon running at 27 that was just a ridiculous time, and now at 43 I go sub 3, it's just mind blowing to me."

Amazingly, Dave was not finished there. He has continued working with our training approaches and continues to improve year after year. Since his breakthrough 2:57 performance, Dave has run many more sub-3-hour marathons, including his current personal record of 2:54.

Dave is an amazing example of how, through dedication, consistency, and the proper training approach, an athlete can not only become faster after forty, but can take his performance to a truly elite level.

» Racing Strategies and Mental Approaches

Life's battles don't always go to the strongest or fastest man, but sooner or later the man who wins is the fellow who thinks he can. —STEVE PREFONTAINE

Your training program may have you in the best marathon form of your life, but if you execute a flawed racing strategy or have a poor mental approach, you will likely fall short of your goals. This chapter will present powerful racing strategies and mental approaches that put the icing on the cake of any marathon training program.

PACING

Pacing is absolutely key to marathon success. In fact, we train athletes for all types of endurance sports competitions, and there is no sport in which pacing is more important than the marathon. Not only should an athlete have a specific pacing strategy for a certain race, but his marathon training program should also be built around this particular pacing strategy. In other words, our training plan should be fully supportive of our ability to run the pace or paces we plan to run on race day. Our pacing strategy and training plan must be fully integrated.

Should you run an even pace all the way? Should you go out fast and "bank some time"? Or should you perhaps "negative split"; that is, run the second half of the marathon faster than the first half? In the following sections we will explain these and other strategies and approaches, the pros and cons of each, and help you to select the optimal one for you.

>> "Banking Time"

The most common error in marathoning, and endurance sports in general, is going out too fast, or in other words, running too fast in the early stages of the race. Athletes have a certain pace and race plan in mind, but then the starting gun goes off and instantly it goes out the window.

It's a strange phenomenon, but if you have experienced it, you know exactly what we mean. There is a feeling that often comes over an athlete at the start of a race. It's almost euphoric. All of a sudden that pace we had planned on in training—the one we were not sure we could actually maintain for 26.2 miles—now feels ridiculously easy. We find ourselves running along with other runners at a faster pace, and it seems as if we could maintain it all day.

We are not psychologists, but our guess is that this is based on several factors. For one, we are tapered, fueled, hydrated, and rested. As a result, we actually do feel a lot better than we do normally. After this, however, the reasons all seem to be mental. We are excited to be in the race, and after training diligently for so long, it's a wonderful relief to hear the starter's gun go off and finally experience the race we have spent months anticipating. Other athletes are running right there alongside you—you can feel their positive energy—and they seem to just pull you along with them.

Then you go through the first mile marker and see your first mile split. (This, by the way, is a key point in the race for the athlete who goes out too fast. There is still time to save your race if you take immediate action and return to your original planned pace.) But say the pace you see is 30 seconds faster than what was planned. This is exciting—you never thought that particular pace could feel so good! You know the right thing to do is back off that pace immediately and get back on your plan. But it feels so good, and the other runners around you seem to feel the same way. So you keep going.

You also think that even if you do eventually end up having to slow down, at least you will have "banked" a significant amount of time. You will get so far ahead of your goal time that even if you need to slow down, you will still make your goal with minutes to spare.

This excitement usually continues to a point around the 10K mark, where you may find yourself 2 or 3 minutes faster than planned. Here's where you start to get a sinking feeling that this may not have been a smart idea. By the halfway point you are sure it was a bad idea, and you wonder how you can possibly keep this pace up, or anything close to it, for another half marathon. By the time you go through the 20-mile mark, you swear there's a piano on your back, and you are so exhausted you are not even tracking your time anymore. All you can do is focus on putting one foot in front of the other and hope that you can still finish without embarrassing yourself more than you already have.

This is where the old "4–1" rule applies. For every second per mile faster than Target Marathon Pace you run in the first 10K of the race, you will give back up to 4 seconds per mile in the final 10K of the race. Having trained hundreds of athletes over the years, amazingly the 4–1 rule holds true time and again if the athlete goes out too fast in the early stages of the race.

For the vast majority of marathoners, an even pace is the best way to run a marathon. As discussed in the first chapter, we can use the Three Magic Bullets sessions not only to train for a specific Target Marathon Pace, but also to determine, based on our training results, whether or not we are ready and fit enough to achieve our goal.

>> Just a Little Cushion

For most athletes, our suggestion is to build in a small 2- to 3-minute cushion under your marathon goal. Not a major "banking" of time, just a small cushion of about 5 to 7 seconds extra per mile to cover any issues that may arise during the marathon. This can help with so many situations, such as needing to stop briefly to go to the bathroom, missing a handoff at the aid station and needing to quickly stop or go back, or just not hitting your fueling and hydration as well as you wanted to and, as a result, slowing down a little over the final few miles.

As an example, say an athlete wants to break 3 hours for his marathon. Just squeaking below 3 hours equates to an average pace of 6:51 minutes per mile. Instead of training with this pace and actually running the race with this pace, the approach we would suggest is to build a slight cushion into this time, both in training and in the race itself. A better pace to work with might be 6:45 minutes per mile. It is 6 seconds per mile faster and equates to a marathon time just under 2:57, thus allowing for a 3-minute cushion.

This athlete would target 6:45 minutes per mile in his Marathon Pacing Sessions and base his Higher-Intensity Repeats and Long Runs off this pace as explained in the Three Magic Bullets in

Chapter 1. Specifically, he would target his Higher-Intensity Repeats at 30 seconds per mile faster than this pace, and his Long Runs at 30 to 60 seconds slower than this pace. For this example, his pace would equate to 6:15 minutes per mile or faster for the Higher-Intensity Repeats and 7:15 to 7:45 minutes per mile for the Long Runs.

If he is able to maintain these paces throughout his sixteen-week marathon training program, it indicates he is ready to achieve his goal. And even if there are some issues or problems during the race, he will be pacing himself in a way that permits him to gradually build up a 3-minute cushion so he may still achieve his target time. If he has no issues and experiences a near-perfect race, he may very well end up achieving his goal with a couple of minutes to spare.

Another advantage of targeting an even pace with a slight cushion built in is that it's an approach that works well with pace groups. Many marathons offer prearranged pace groups. Typically, a pace group has a leader who will be running a specific pace, and any runners who want to run that same pace merely run along with him. Usually the pace group leaders wear a sign with their target time on it so they can be easily sighted. Joining a pace group is a helpful way to achieve your marathon time goal, and preparing in training to run a specific, even pace on race day fits in perfectly with a pace group approach.

» Negative Splitting

One of the most talked-about approaches to marathon pacing is negative splitting. This simply means you either run the second half of the marathon faster than the first, or you gradually increase your pace as the race progresses. If executed properly, this approach allows the runner to conserve more of his glycogen stores for later in the race when he needs them most.

Does it work? Yes. The problem with this strategy, however, is that few runners can do it. Negative splitting is a fairly advanced technique. It usually takes an experienced athlete with a great deal of feel for his exact pace and the discipline to stick with his plan. As mentioned above, the vast majority of athletes are prone to going out too fast, rather than too slow.

Having said this, we would not discourage any athlete from trying this, especially faster marathoners who have already brought their times down and are looking to improve even more. Our suggestion is not to vary your pace greatly from the first half to the second half of the marathon. We are talking about a fairly subtle adjustment, perhaps 10 seconds per mile.

To use the example of the athlete who wants to run a sub-3-hour marathon (average pace of about 6:51 minutes per mile), a possible negative splitting strategy would maintain a 6:55 minute-per-mile pace for the first half and then a lowered 6:45 pace on the second half. This equates to a blended pace of 6:50, which equals a 2:59.02 marathon.

» Run/Walk Approach

Elite marathoner, coach, and author Jeff Galloway has popularized the run/walk approach to marathons. This strategy is simply to take short, periodic walking breaks throughout the marathon to freshen up the legs, and then return to running. Many marathoners, at all levels of performance, have had success with some version of a run/walk approach.

One common run/walk strategy is to walk for 10 seconds, or some other brief predetermined amount of time, at each aid station. Not only does this accomplish the goal of quickly freshening up the legs, but it also makes it easier to accomplish your fueling and hydration plan at the aid station, without spilling or dropping anything. Another common approach is to walk for a predetermined amount of time at each mile marker. Most of the faster marathoners who utilize this approach keep the walk segments very brief, but as a marathoner's projected finishing time gets longer, extended walk segments of up to a minute or so per aid station or per mile may be optimal, depending on the athlete.

We know many athletes who say they are a little afraid of this approach because they think they may not be able to start running again once they start to walk. The best way to determine if this is a good approach for you is to test it out several times in training during your Long Runs. Try different amounts of time for your walking breaks, from 10 to 60 seconds, and see if it makes you feel faster overall. Just be sure to keep your walk breaks on the same time schedule throughout the run, and begin taking them right from the start (i.e., don't wait until you are tired to begin walk breaks). This may or may not be the approach for you. But you won't know for sure unless you give it a try in training.

MENTAL APPROACHES

As important as pacing is to marathon success, there is also a large mental component. We are often amused by the questions we receive from well-meaning people who are not endurance athletes and don't know much about it. One of the most common is, "What do you think about when you are out there running for so long?"

This is actually an important question for all of us to consider. One of the greatest attributes we have observed in many of the elite athletes we have worked with is their ability to control their thoughts. Some athletes control their thoughts, while others let their thoughts control them.

» It's a Sport about Not Quitting

Don started competitive running many years ago as a high school cross-country harrier. It concerned him then that he would frequently think about quitting when the going got tough. He would be racing his hardest and suffering through the middle stages of the race, where he would think about quitting. Not because he was injured, but because it seemed so hard and he had self-doubts. He never did quit, but he definitely did think about it. Fortunately for him, a top endurance athlete at the time, whom he greatly admired, assured him with a big smile, "If you don't think about quitting at least three times during a race, then you aren't running hard enough."

This came as a great relief to Don. He was not the only one who thought about quitting; even the best athletes did, too. This experience helped him to understand the true nature of endurance sports and provided a philosophy for success that has served him well for decades since.

Ultimately, endurance sports are not about beating the other guy. Endurance sports are about not quitting. It sounds a little crazy, but that's what it's all about. We choose a distance and a time in which we want to complete that distance, and then we go for it. It's all about persistence in reaching a goal, or stated another way, it's all about not quitting. Your competition is never some other person; your competition is always yourself and your thoughts.

This realization was a revelation to Don, and it has led him to so many positive outcomes. By understanding and truly accepting the notion that endurance sports are all about your ability to control your thoughts and resist the urge to quit, a huge competitive burden is removed. You start to view the sport in an entirely new way.

Don reached a point in his own career as an elite age-group athlete where he was so unfocused on his competitors he did not even know whom he was racing against. Early in his career he would check who was racing before the start and keep those competitors in mind during the race. That all changed when he sincerely didn't see them as competitors anymore. He learned to have his goal and his race plan, and it did not involve anyone else. He used to get a kick out of it when, at some major race like the Hawaii Ironman, someone would ask him on race morning about his competition. He would smile and respond, "The 8-inch space between my two ears." The confused looks he often received were so funny, it would help him to relax even more prior to the race. But the reality is that his response was honest. No one in the race was going to determine his success or failure that day except him.

›› False Confidence

Again, we are not psychologists, so what we say on this topic is based purely on our experiences as athletes and coaches for many years. But we are not big fans of a lot of the positive-thinking techniques out there. Looking at yourself in the mirror and repeating, "I am the best," does not make it true. In reality, the fact that you know it's not true will ultimately work against you. You will undermine yourself.

True confidence is created through consistency, humility, and building on success. We need to have a great coach and/or a great training plan and consistently work with it over time. We need to accept our mistakes and weaknesses as learning opportunities, and we need to embrace our successes, no matter how small, and allow ourselves to enjoy them.

We often refer to this mind-set as the "Humble Happy Warrior." Many of our coached athletes have had tremendous success with this approach. Those who have been able to embrace it, and become it, have often broken through to new levels of performance. And even more importantly, they learned to enjoy their sport much more. They gradually grew to become confident, calm, and very successful athletes.

» The 10-10-6 Approach: Relaxation-Focus-Competitive

What should we think about during the race? One of the most successful road-racing strategies we have worked on with our coached athletes over the years is our "Relaxation-Focus-Competitive" approach. When applied specifically to the marathon, we often refer to it as simply the "10-10-6" approach.

Following is an example of how this mental approach applies to the marathon:

- **Relaxation Phase (miles 0 through 10):** Your mind-set for the first 10 miles should be relaxation. Hitting your target pace at each mile marker should be relatively easy if you have trained properly. So you just want to get into your predetermined pace and feel as relaxed as possible. Push aside any thoughts of competition. Think of the runners around you as your good friends who are out for a fun training run together. Visualize yourself being pulled along almost effortlessly by the crowd. Don't think ahead. Live in the moment and keep hitting your pace and following your fueling and hydration plan.

- **Focus Phase (miles 11 through 20):** Your mind-set should now shift slightly to one of focus. You want to stay extra-sharp mentally now as things become gradually more challenging. You want to eliminate any possible mistakes in pacing, fueling, and hydration and think ahead to each mile marker, each aid station, and each predetermined fuel and hydration time. You want to stay as relaxed as possible, but also start thinking of your overall race plan as broken down into a specific sequence of individual tasks: checking your pace at each mile marker, drinking a specific number of ounces of an energy drink at each aid station, consuming your energy gels every 30 minutes as planned, etc.

- **Competitive Phase (miles 21 through 26.2):** This is the "racing part" of your race. Now is the time to finally let those competitive juices flow. Spot athletes up ahead and work to catch and pass them. Stick with your plan in terms of fueling and hydration, but if you think you can pick up the pace at all, now is the time to challenge yourself to gradually do so. Reflect on all the training you have done to get to this point, and fight with all your spirit to get through this final 10K and to the finish line as fast as you can.

This approach to marathoning fits in well with our overall approach to training, and many of our coached athletes have had great success with it over the years. Give it a try in your next marathon.

» Posting Goals

One of the most effective techniques we have used with our athletes over the years is posting goals. What we mean by posting goals is to make up a little sign with your race time goal on it and post it in a few key places where you will see it every day throughout your sixteen-week marathon training program. Make sure it is in a place where you will see it several times a day. It doesn't sound like much, but this is a powerful technique for success.

The bathroom mirror is a great place to post your goals. It is often the first place you look in the morning and the last at night. Another good place is somewhere in your office or on your desk. A third possibility is in an area where you frequently work out—perhaps where you can see it from a treadmill. Another good place is as a screen saver.

» PERSONAL BEST

Carl Curran is profiled in Chapter 3 of this book. Don recently coached him for both the Boston and Chicago Marathons in the same year. Carl got off to a great start and after first running a personal best time of 3:05 at Boston, both he and Don felt he was ready to achieve his goal of a sub-3-hour marathon. On the day after Boston, Don suggested to Carl that he post a simple little sign on his bathroom mirror for the next twenty-four weeks leading up to the Chicago Marathon. The sign read "2:57 Chicago." It was surely a sweet feeling for Carl twenty-four weeks later when he took down his little sign on the day after the Chicago Marathon—after running his new personal best marathon time of 2:57.

While some of these places will be private (like your bathroom), some will be more public (like your office). This is fine. Don't be embarrassed if people ask you about your goal. If they do, just give them the straight answer: "That's my goal time for my marathon coming up in a few weeks." The very act of saying this aloud can be very powerful. Every time we explain our goal to someone, we find we become even more determined to achieve it.

You should post your goal right at the beginning of your sixteen-week marathon training plan, so it is there to support you all the way. It's amazing how much impact this will have during your training. Often an athlete tells us that they believed the goal was a stretch when they first posted it, but by the time the race came around, they felt that it was pretty much a "done deal."

If you plan to run some practice races as part of your marathon preparation, it can be a powerful technique to make separate signs for each of these races as well, and to remove them one at a time after completing each race:

- 3:30 Marathon

- 1:41 Half Marathon

- 45:00 10K

Not only does this technique help you to focus on your goals, but it also creates a pattern of success in your mind. Your confidence will grow as you close in on your ultimate goal. Surely after clicking off the 10K goal and the half marathon goal, you will be highly confident that you can achieve your marathon goal.

» Positive Affirmation Game

We need to develop positive self-talk. As mentioned earlier in this chapter, we don't believe the way to do that is to stare at yourself in the mirror and repeat, "I am the best," or words to that effect. This is false confidence, and it will crumble when the race gets tough. But we all have many positive attributes mixed right in with all of our flaws. It is important that we remember this and think about ourselves in a positive way. We can't berate ourselves for our faults and ignore our strengths, and somehow think this is a formula for success. We want to build on our strengths as we work on improving our weaknesses. Overall, we want both our strengths and weaknesses to gradually keep improving and heading in a positive direction.

A great way to get out of the habit of negative self-talk is with the "positive affirmation game." You need to play the game with another person—someone who is close to you and wants to accomplish goals and improve himself just as you do. This can be your spouse, a good friend, a regular training partner, or perhaps someone you work with. The way the game is played is that every time you catch your partner saying something negative about himself, you have to call him on it and require him to say three positive things instead. The three things need to be true and they need to be said in a sincere tone. No sarcasm allowed. You can pick a period of time to play the game—the longer the better—and you can keep score.

We started out doing this years ago, and not only did it help us both become more positive, but gradually the game aspect faded away and it just became the way we talk with each other, and others as well. More important than how it made us talk, it became the way we think.

» ED MCENTEE:
40-Plus Athlete Success Story

Ed McEntee is an engineer, owner of his own company, and married with two adult children. Ed has been a competitive runner for more than twenty years and has completed more than ten marathons. Ed's fastest marathon time prior to turning forty had been a 3:58, but he has since become significantly faster. In fact, at the age of forty-nine, Ed recorded a time of 3:25, which qualified him yet again for the Boston Marathon.

Ed credits his success to effective training with the Three Magic Bullets sessions. In addition, Ed has become leaner and stronger through an overall weight management and functional strength program, thus improving his power-to-weight ratio. Ed has also improved other elements of his marathon game, including his marathon pacing, as well as his fueling and hydration. He has become a more complete marathoner.

This is all somewhat ironic, as the marathon was never a distance Ed McEntee enjoyed. In fact, it was his least favorite road race. He particularly enjoys the challenge of the marathon distance now and is running marathons more than 30 minutes faster than when he was under forty—and his times continue to improve.

» Avoiding Common Training and Racing Mistakes

It is a rough road that leads to the heights of greatness. —SENECA

Eliminating mistakes is one of the most important elements for marathon success. It is so easy to go off track, and there are usually so many well-meaning friends and other training resources ready and willing to offer you the wrong advice at the wrong time. It's easy to fall prey to this because there are so many counterintuitive aspects to training and racing—ideas and suggestions that seem totally logical, but are almost sure to spoil your marathon journey. One of the frustrating things about all these little traps is that unsuspecting athletes continually step into them time and time again.

Avoiding these traps is especially important for the forty-plus athlete, who has less ability to bounce back from a mistake. The veteran athlete needs to rely more on racing and training smarts than on raw athletic ability, and this chapter will help you to accomplish this. We will present ten of the most common training and racing mistakes and how to avoid them. We'll start with five of the most common racing mistakes and then discuss five of the most common training mistakes.

FIVE COMMON RACING MISTAKES TO AVOID

Five common racing mistakes are the following:

1. Going Out Too Fast
2. Not Running "Your Own Race"
3. Not Fueling and Hydrating Properly
4. Racing in New Shoes
5. Not Planning for Weather Conditions

»» 1. Going Out Too Fast

The most common marathon racing mistake is going out too fast. In fact, it's not just the number one marathon mistake, it's the number one mistake for all types of endurance competitions.

As discussed in the "Pacing" section in Chapter 11, something strange often happens to athletes at the start of a race: A euphoric feeling descends on them, and the pace they had prepared for in training all of a sudden feels much easier than it ever did before. As a result, the race plan gets thrown out the window and the runner starts off much faster than planned. Sooner or later this exuberance comes back to haunt him, and by the later stages of the marathon, he cannot even come close to his original target pace, let alone a new target pace decided on during the early race euphoria.

As discussed in "The Importance of Proper Fueling" in Chapter 7, our bodies have a very limited ability to store sugar in the form of glycogen, which is one of our key fuels. If we go too fast too early in the race, we use up our glycogen. Later in the race, when we need it most, we no longer have glycogen in the quantities needed to maintain our desired pace.

For the vast majority of marathoners, either a consistently even pace or a slightly slower pace in the first half of the marathon and a faster pace in the second half are the best strategies. These strategies are discussed in greater detail under "Pacing" in Chapter 11.

You want to hold back a little in the first mile and check your time at the very first mile marker. As soon as you know your pace, you can make whatever adjustment is necessary to start hitting your mile markers right on your predetermined pace. There are many ways to do this. Some athletes like to run with a GPS to get immediate feedback on their pace, which enables them to make continual adjustments. Others wear a wristband with their targeted mile splits printed on it. Some races offer prearranged pace groups that allow you to join up with a group of runners who plan to run the same pace as you. These are all successful ways to ensure that you can maintain your target pace.

>> 2. Not Running "Your Own Race"

Another common racing mistake is not sticking to your plan and instead running someone else's race. An athlete often finds himself shoulder to shoulder with another athlete in the early stages of a race. After a couple of miles of this, the athlete begins to see the other athlete as "the competition" and starts to race the person. He picks up the pace a little to beat him to the next turn, then again on a hill to see if he can "drop him," and then starts to use race tactics that have nothing to do with where he is in the race.

All of these distractions just throw you off your pace and away from your race plan. We once witnessed an athlete go through the 6-mile mark of a marathon 1 minute ahead of plan and then proceed to pick it up even more to "shake the guy" he was racing. This is an absolute race killer. In fact, both of the runners engaged in these tactics so early in the race are almost certain to ruin their days.

We like to tell our coached athletes that they are not racing anyone prior to the 20-mile mark in the marathon, because the race doesn't even start until the final 10K. Until then, your only competition is in the space between your ears. You should be solely focused on your pace, your plan, and your race. If you are with a pace group, or another runner happens to be running along with you at the same pace, don't see him as your competitor. If anything, see his presence as helpful, and mentally visualize him pulling you along at *your* pace. If his pace changes, then let him go. It's as simple as that. If you hold your pace through 20 miles and are pleased to find yourself feeling surprisingly strong and energized, then this is the time to very gradually pick up the pace and begin looking ahead to the process of trying to "run down" your competitors.

See our "Relaxation-Focus-Competitive" approach to racing, which is presented under "Mental Approaches" in Chapter 11. We refer to this approach as "10-10-6" when applied specifically to the marathon. This approach can be immensely helpful in preventing you from making the common mistake of "not running your own race."

>> 3. Not Fueling and Hydrating Properly

No matter how perfect your training program and race plan, it's virtually worthless if you do not properly fuel and hydrate before and during your race. This is such an important element to success, and it is so often missed by marathoners, that we have dedicated an entire chapter to it in this book (see Chapter 7, "Fuel and Hydrate Like You Mean It").

The title comes from talking to so many disappointed athletes over the years who believed that they had done everything correctly in their training and strategy and approach on race day. But despite their thorough preparation, they fell significantly short of their marathon goal.

As we helped them analyze their disappointing race, assuming that their pacing was on target as planned, the next area to come to mind would be fueling and hydration. We would ask and usually get an answer like, "Well, I think I could have done a little better with that." After a little more probing, we would have to agree. In fact, we usually concluded that they could have done a *lot* better with their fueling and hydration.

After identifying fueling and hydration as the issue, we often would tell the athlete, "If you are really serious about achieving your marathon goal, my friend, you need to fuel and hydrate like you mean it." Take this important aspect of marathoning to heart, consider the tips and tools in Chapter 7, and put together the optimal fueling and hydration plan to ensure your marathon success.

» 4. Racing in New Shoes

After training consistently for sixteen weeks, our marathon is finally next weekend. Time to get some fast new racing shoes for the big day . . . right?

Wrong! A fresh pair of shoes may look great, but until they are properly broken in, they are not good for racing. The chance of the shoes causing blisters or some other issue is far too great. Our suggestion is only race in shoes that you have been running in regularly for at least three to four weeks.

Most marathoners will race in either their regular training shoes or lightweight training shoes, and this is the smart thing to do. Training shoes should be changed about every 500 miles. So depending on the amount of actual running you do, as opposed to cross-training, a new pair of running shoes may or may not get you through a sixteen-week marathon training cycle.

A great tip is to have two pairs of shoes going at the same time. Start with two fresh pairs at the start of your marathon cycle and then rotate them on training runs throughout the sixteen-week cycle. In addition to being sure you will have a comfortable pair of shoes ready to go for your marathon, there are many other advantages of rotating two pairs, including having an extra day to dry out your shoes when they get wet.

Only the fastest marathoners can benefit from racing the marathon in racing flats. There are many theories on the cutoff for this, but we generally suggest that if your target pace is under 7 minutes per mile, you could probably benefit from using racing flats. Otherwise, you should race in either lightweight trainers or your regular training shoes.

Since we wear racing flats or light trainers less frequently, it's even more important to plan ahead to be sure they are properly broken in prior to the race. Our suggestion would be to wear them at least once a week in training during the last six weeks leading up to the race and, of course, in any tune-up race you plan to do during your marathon training cycle.

In general, you should not change anything in the last days leading up to your race. Everything should be thoroughly tested and rehearsed during training. Race clothing, fueling and hydration sources, pre-race routine . . . you name it, every detail should be completely vetted and nailed down well in advance of your race.

›› 5. Not Planning for Weather Conditions

Another common racing error is not being prepared for the weather conditions. Athletes often go to a race with certain weather conditions in mind, only to find that the actual race conditions are far different. We have been to so many races over the years where the temperature was expected to be in the fifties and was actually in the thirties; and even more often where it was supposed to be in the fifties and ended up in the eighties. It happens all the time. Don't assume the race conditions will be the same as the prior year. Go to the race prepared for several different weather scenarios.

Don't be that crazy guy at the marathon expo who learns of the unexpected cold front coming in the next day and tries frantically to find suitable racing clothes. This is the guy who has been diligently following his training program and has made countless sacrifices in virtually all areas of his life for the past sixteen weeks. And now, with only hours to go before the start, he doesn't even have the right clothes to race in.

Pack race clothing for your "likely weather scenario," your "hotter than expected weather scenario," and your "cooler than expected weather scenario." There really is no excuse for not doing this. The equipment needed to do road races is pretty light compared to triathlon and other sports. To be prepared with clothing and equipment for different weather conditions is really easy to do and can make the difference between achieving and not achieving your goals.

The rule of thumb we always use for a marathon is to dress as if it is 10 degrees warmer than it actually is. You may feel a little cool in the first 10K of the race, but after that you will be very glad that you dressed as lightly as you did.

A great trick for marathoning is to wear a warm hat and gloves (or just socks on your hands) at the start. Then be prepared to drop them at an aid station or hand them to a friend at a predetermined spot on the course, if you decide you don't need them anymore. We are often negatively affected by the cold, so we frequently race this way. Once we feel warmed up, however, we will usually hand them off to a friend or leave them at an aid station along the course.

What if you live in a relatively cool climate and you will be traveling to race a marathon in a much warmer climate? In this situation, not only should you dress appropriately for the weather, but you should also consider incorporating heat acclimation techniques into your training. In other words, you want to simulate hotter conditions in training so that your body can adapt to hotter and more humid conditions.

We have raced in Hawaii many times over the years, even though we live in the northeastern United States. Whenever possible, we arrive in Hawaii one to two weeks ahead of our event so we can fully acclimate to the hot, humid climate. Of course, this is not always possible to do, however, and most athletes are lucky if they can spare the time to arrive at the race location two or three days in advance.

If this is your situation, you should take specific steps in your training to simulate warmer conditions. The most popular technique is to wear extra layers of clothing while training. This is good, but by far the number one trick we recommend for heat acclimation is to wear a wool stretch cap while running. A large amount of our body heat escapes through our head, so by wearing a wool stretch cap, we can trap much of this heat. This simulates the effects of running in extremely hot conditions. (Tip: Always increase hydration accordingly when running in either actual hot conditions or simulated hot conditions.)

FIVE COMMON TRAINING MISTAKES TO AVOID

Five common training mistakes are the following:

1. Overtraining
2. Straying from Your Training Plan
3. Insufficient Sleep and Rest
4. Playing "Catch-Up"
5. Not Tapering Properly

≫ 1. Overtraining

More often than not, what most athletes refer to as "overtraining" might better be described as "too much too soon." It's not really that the volume of training was too much; it's more that the athlete increased to that volume too quickly.

The human body is amazing in how it can adapt to training and grow stronger and faster. Yet it's important to understand that your body has a unique rate at which it can adapt. If we increase training volume too quickly, it won't adapt, but will instead break down. This is the principle of gradual adaptation. If we do the proper training and increase it at the correct rate, our bodies will absorb it and grow stronger and faster. As discussed in Chapter 2, "The Recovery Trick," this period of adaptation tends to slow as we get older.

So many injuries occur because athletes do not respect this principle. They take a mind-over-matter approach to their training and, through sheer force of will, aggressively train and force their bodies into the condition they want. This absolutely does not work. If your body is not ready to accept a change, it will break down.

The smart athlete always works with his body, not against it. Training needs to start out gradually and build at a modest rate of increase. As a general guideline for marathon training, our suggestion is to increase your combined weekly training durations by no more than 1 hour per week, after building your total combined weekly durations up to at least 3.5 hours. Prior to building up to 3.5 hours per week, our suggestion is to limit weekly increases to no more than 30 to 45 minutes.

Recently a newbie runner planning to do her first marathon told us she was going to do a 20-mile training run with the local running club that weekend. She was nervous because she had never run more than an hour before, but she felt it was time to "step it up" for the marathon. Based on her pace for a one-hour run, it appeared likely that she would be lucky to complete a 20-mile run in less than four hours. We asked her if this sounded sensible to her—the fact that she was about to run for four hours despite having never run for more than an hour. She said of course it was—all runners training for a marathon do 20-mile runs.

We hope we talked her out of that run. It was not that a 20-miler was not something she should attempt, but it was simply too much too soon. At best, it would have been "junk training," and at worst, it might have resulted in an injury, putting an early end to her marathon goal.

›› 2. Straying from Your Training Program

Find a coach you trust and then follow his or her plan as closely as possible. Talk to your coach if you feel the need to change the plan by adding some things to it or taking other things away. In a good plan, every workout has a purpose and is scheduled in a specific order to bring about a desired result. Any time you change one piece, you run the risk of negatively affecting the intended results for other days in the week, if not the entire week. As we like to say about a perfectly arranged training week: "Everything relates to everything."

As a simple example, say your program has the following workouts planned for Monday through Thursday (see the "Explanation of Training Plan Abbreviations" sidebar in Chapter 5):

- Monday: Moderate 60-minute Z1 to Z2 run

- Tuesday: 1-mile warm-up, then 8 x 800 meters Z4 @ 400 meter jog, then 1-mile cooldown

- Wednesday: Moderate 60-minute Z1 to Z2 run

- Thursday: 1-mile warm-up, then 60 minutes at Target Marathon Pace, then 1-mile cooldown

The athlete surmises that if completing the Monday and Wednesday runs at a moderate perceived effort is good, then running them at a faster perceived effort must be even better. So he instead runs the Monday moderate run at about a 90 percent perceived effort. On Tuesday, the athlete tries to run the planned Higher-Intensity Repeats, but is very disappointed at how sluggish he feels and how slow he runs. He is not even able to raise his heart rate up into Z4. Then on Wednesday, the athlete "makes up" for Tuesday's poor workout by again running the moderate run at a 90 percent perceived effort. Once again, on Thursday the athlete is sluggish and unable to hold his Target Marathon Pace for the full 60 minutes.

The athlete contacts his coach to let him know how frustrated he is and how the training plan does not seem to be working. What the athlete doesn't understand is that by going too hard on his moderate aerobic days, he is unable to go hard enough on his higher-intensity days. Had the athlete backed off and completed the Monday and Wednesday moderate runs at a comfortable pace, he would have been successful hitting his paces on his Tuesday Higher-Intensity Repeats and Thursday Marathon Pacing Session. He would have experienced an exceptional week of training and gained great confidence from the workouts. Instead, the athlete had what we like to refer to as a "junk training week," and he lost confidence in both himself and his training plan.

The moral of the story is to trust your coach and trust your plan. Follow both as closely as you can, and don't try to overly "fix" or "improve" the plan as you go. If you lose confidence in your plan, then you need a new plan.

» 3. Insufficient Sleep and Rest

The importance of sleep and rest is highly underestimated by most athletes. In fact, when trying to be there for your family, pursue a successful career, and run a fast marathon, if something has to go, sleep is usually the first casualty.

The problem is that sleep is required for your body to fully absorb the benefits of training. In fact, a basic synergy of training is that you challenge your body in a certain way and it responds by building back stronger and faster. When does this building-back process take place? It takes place mostly while you sleep.

So after you run that 20-mile training session, it is not until you have slept and built back stronger that the workout has been completed. It would be more accurate to say that the workout is over the next morning, when you wake up, than it is to say it's over when you stop running.

Don't waste that great 20-mile training run by going out late that evening and then getting only four hours of sleep. Much of the training benefit of the run will not be absorbed by your body. Much of your hard work will be squandered. What's more, you may become more susceptible to injury or illness due to a weakened immune system.

While in marathon training, and for general good health purposes, we suggest seven to eight hours of sleep per night for our coached athletes.

》 4. Playing "Catch-Up"

It is easy to miss a workout in your training plan due to some unforeseen situation that arises during your day. This is why most marathoners prefer to get their workouts done first thing in the morning. Not only is it a wonderful and positive way to start the day, but if you plan to fit your workout in first thing, there is less chance that something that comes up during the day derails your training plans. Computers go down, trains run off schedule, bosses ask you to work late—you name it, it happens. By running first thing, the chance of getting in your training every day is greatly increased.

But what if you don't? What if you miss a workout? What should you do?

Many athletes try to play catch-up by doubling up on workouts the next day. Typically we see athletes do the missed workout in the morning and the scheduled workout in the evening. In general, this is not a good idea. Doing double workouts in a single day is not safe or productive for most over-forty athletes. Sure, you may be able to get away with this once in a while, but the risk is far greater than the reward. The recovery time in between workouts is important, and the chance of injury increases greatly when you double up on workouts.

What we like to suggest to our coached athletes is to "slide it, flip it, or skip it." For example, say the athlete has the following training schedule for three days and unfortunately, for reasons out of her control, is unable to work out on Friday. What should she do?

Friday: 60-minute Moderate Aerobic Run
Saturday: 20-mile Long Run
Sunday: Rest Day

In priority order, we would suggest the following:

- **Slide it:** Slide everything forward by one day. Do Friday's 60-minute run on Saturday, Saturday's 20-mile run on Sunday, and return to the schedule on Monday.

- **Flip it:** If you only have time to do the 20-mile run on Saturday, keep it there and flip Friday and Sunday. In other words, declare Friday your rest day and do the 60-minute moderate run on Sunday.

- **Skip it:** What if the only day you have enough time to do the 20-mile run is Saturday and you don't have any time to train on Sunday? Then skip it. Do Saturday and Sunday as planned and then go into the next week. No single missed workout is going to ruin your marathon plan. Let it go and move on.

» 5. Not Tapering Properly

As discussed in the sixteen-week marathon training programs in Chapter 5, each has significant three-week tapers prior to the marathon. It is crucial that after all of your hard training, you have the proper amount of time to recover, get rested, and as we like to say to our coached athletes, "get race sharp."

The beauty of a perfect taper is that it gradually reduces training volume at just the right rate, so your body recovers without losing fitness. If your volume is too much during the taper, you will not recover sufficiently and you will take all that fatigue into the race with you. If, on the other hand, you taper too much, you will lose fitness at the same time you are getting rested. To tell you the truth, however, in all our years of coaching, we can't ever remember an athlete who tapered too much. It just doesn't seem to be in the marathoner's mental makeup.

Many athletes find the concept of tapering difficult to accept, and they continue to train hard right up until race time. This of course leads to a subpar performance because they are not sufficiently rested to achieve a peak performance. Why do so many athletes blow their race in the taper?

It relates to the "no pain, no gain" and "more is always better" philosophies discussed throughout this book. In the case of the former, the athlete thinks, "Tapering does not hurt enough, therefore it cannot be good," and in the latter, "If my coach says running X amount during the taper phase is good, then running three times X amount must be better."

If you can relate to either of these mind-sets, it really helps to have a good coach to talk you down in these situations, because nothing is going to ruin your race more than a poor taper. Follow your plan and your coach's advice closely during your taper, and don't let your emotions get the best of you. Trust in your plan and strive to have a perfect taper.

One other taper tip: Don't try anything new. We discussed the risk of getting new shoes, but this holds true for all the other variables as well: fueling and hydration sources, nutrition, race clothing, stretching routine, core and strength routine, massage, etc. Stick with what you know and what you have thoroughly tested in training. The taper is not the time for experimentation.

13

» *Iron-Distance Marathon Secrets*

Most people run a race to see who is fastest.
I run a race to see who has the most guts.
—STEVE PREFONTAINE

This chapter is for you triathletes, and aspiring triathletes, who want to run successful marathons within an Iron-Distance triathlon.

The Iron-Distance triathlon consists of 2.4 miles (3.8 km) of swimming, followed by 112 miles (180 km) of cycling, and then a full 26.2-mile (42.2 km) marathon run. Many athletes make the mistake of assuming that you prepare for the marathon within an Iron-Distance triathlon in much the same way as you prepare for a straight marathon. Furthermore, they expect to be able to run the same time, or at least one that's pretty close.

The reality is that preparing to run a marathon after you have completed 2.4 miles of swimming and 112 miles of cycling is very different. This chapter will explain the difference and provide helpful tips and guidance on how to run faster marathons within Iron-Distance triathlons.

First, it's important to point out that one of the most alluring elements of the Iron-Distance triathlon, and what makes it so popular, is the fact that it concludes with a full marathon. The reason this is so exciting to many is that there was a time not very long ago when the marathon was considered to be the most challenging endurance event possible. In fact, at the time, many openly wondered if the human body could even complete such an event.

As recently as the 1970s, only elite road racers would attempt marathons. Quite the opposite of what we see today, with literally millions of regular people participating. As amazing as it sounds, it was not until 1980 that the marathon was even included in the Olympics for women. We guess someone thought women were not strong enough to participate. This seems funny today when we see the enormously successful performances of women in both the marathon and the Iron-Distance triathlon.

Today, not only do thousands of regular people compete in Iron-Distance triathlons, but these athletes want to get faster, and in no area is this truer than with the Iron-Distance marathon.

FRUSTRATED MARATHONERS

So many marathoners decide to pursue the Iron-Distance dream. While they expect to need to bring their swimming and cycling up to speed, they believe their strong run will also carry them through. More often than not, they become frustrated when they find that they cannot run a marathon within an Iron-Distance triathlon at a pace anywhere close to their personal-record marathon time.

The reason for this is that these are two very different races, and what is required to be successful in each is completely different as well.

As we like to say to our coached athletes, the Iron-Distance triathlon is a finite equation. It's not three races . . . it's just one race. It's not a 2.4-mile race, then a 112-mile race, and then a 26.2-mile race, it's a 140.6-mile race. The effort you exert while cycling has a direct impact on your marathon, and the effort you exert while swimming has a direct impact on both your cycling and your running. Running a marathon fresh and tapered is far different from running a marathon after 2.4 miles of swimming and 112 miles of cycling.

The way to look at it is that we want to optimize the finite equation. We want to hit the optimal level of exertion for each sport that allows us to maximize our overall time for the three sports combined. Going out too hard on the swim will have a direct negative impact on our Iron-Distance marathon performance.

Many will argue back that the swim happens so many hours before the run, how could it possibly affect your run? But it does. It's similar to how in a straight marathon your overall performance will be slowed by going out too fast in the first 5K (see discussion of the "4–1" rule in Chapters 1 and 11).

This fact can frustrate the triathlete because it seems to be very complicated. We are basically saying that to run a fast marathon, one has to first complete the swim and bike at the optimal pace. The triathlete thinks: I am not sure what pace I should be targeting for my marathon. I really have no idea what pace I should be targeting for my swim and bike.

But the answer is simple: heart rate.

PACING RACES VS. HEART-RATE RACES

Marathon training is very much about pacing. As you know, the Three Magic Bullets, which are the key to successful marathon training, are all pace oriented. We have a specific pace or a specific range of paces for each of these key sessions.

Maximizing performance in the Iron-Distance triathlon is not about pacing. It's about heart rate. As we like to guide our coached athletes, some races are "pacing races" and some races are "heart-rate races." The marathon is a great example of a pacing race. It is a race where the best results are achieved through a focus primarily on pace. The Iron-Distance is a great example of a heart rate race. It's a race where the best results are achieved through a focus primarily on heart rate.

This concept can be a difficult one for a lot of experienced marathoners to become comfortable with. Marathoners are so dependent on pace, they are really out of their comfort zone when you advise them to ignore pace and let heart rate dictate how fast they should race.

So what is the heart rate to focus on for an Iron-Distance triathlon? While it varies a little from athlete to athlete, for the vast majority, it is mid-to-high Z2. This simply means the upper half of the Z2 Heart Rate Zone. Sure, if an athlete has more in the tank when they hit the 20-mile marker in the Iron-Distance marathon, they should dig down and push their effort level to the finish. But prior to that, they will usually maximize their overall performance by locking in as close as possible to the upper half of Z2 for the swim, bike, and most of the marathon.

This has enormous implications for how an athlete prepares for an Iron-Distance marathon versus a straight marathon. While the Three Magic Bullets are the key to maximizing an athlete's performance in a straight marathon, the higher-intensity training and pacing work have much less value for the Iron-Distance marathon. This is all about teaching your body to run efficiently in mid-to-high Z2. A little higher-intensity work can help, but is really more of a nice-to-have than a need-to-have element.

We are frequently asked by athletes what pace they should run when they start the marathon within an Iron-Distance triathlon. They are often surprised when we tell them they should be in whatever pace mid-to-high Z2 dictates.

MINUTE-PER-MILE GUIDELINE

After an athlete accepts the proper approach to the Iron-Distance marathon, we are often asked, "Well, if I do follow the mid-to-high Z2 approach to optimize all three sports in the Iron-Distance triathlon, what should I expect my marathon time to be in relation to my straight marathon time?"

Each athlete is unique, and we each have our own strengths and weaknesses, but the best rule of thumb is the "Minute-per-Mile Guideline." Generally, you should be able to run your Iron-Distance marathon at a pace no more than 60 seconds slower per mile than your personal-record marathon pace. This equates to a time of about 26 minutes slower. If you cannot do this, you may be exerting too much effort during the swim and/or bike or you may not be properly preparing for the swim and/or bike. If this appears to be your issue, consider our book *Be Iron Fit, 3rd Edition*, which presents complete Iron-Distance training programs.

We know many elite-level athletes whose Iron-Distance marathons are only about 30 seconds slower per mile. This is rare, however, and most athletes are going to be closer to 60 seconds slower per mile. But that is the range you should consider. You want your Iron-Distance marathon to be about 13 to 26 minutes slower than your straight marathon time. If your time is outside of this range, we suggest you employ some of the approaches we present here.

By the way, does the range of 30 to 60 seconds slower per mile than your straight marathon pace sound familiar to you? It should. That's the target range for the most important of the Three Magic Bullets: the Long Run. So the good news is that by training for the marathon using this book, you will have a good idea of your Iron-Distance marathon pace. Although, as discussed above, your mid-to-high Z2 heart rate will have the final say on race day.

MORE TIPS FOR RUNNING YOUR BEST IRON-DISTANCE MARATHON

Following are five great tips for racing your best Iron-Distance marathon:

- **Avoid Starting Out Too Fast:** It is so easy to come out of the bike-to-run transition to the sound of a cheering crowd and ruin your strong marathon right at the start. We suggest the first thing you focus on coming out of transition is your heart-rate monitor. Find the pace that gets your heart rate into the upper half of Z2 and then focus on holding it there while remaining as relaxed and efficient as you can.

- **Avoid Walking at the Start of the Marathon:** Sure, if you have a health issue, you should not start running. In fact, depending on the issue, you should check in with the medical personnel in the transition area before even heading out on the run course. But if you are healthy, don't make the mistake of telling yourself that you will start walking for a bit before you start to run. Your body starts to go into "recovery mode," and it becomes increasingly tough to get running. If all is well and you are healthy, try to go right into your run and get your body going.

- **Consider the Run/Walk Approach:** Consider the run/walk approach for the marathon, discussed in Chapter 11. This is the approach where you start running right away, but mix in predetermined walk breaks. This freshens up the legs and segments the run nicely from a mental standpoint. The most popular pattern for most of our coached athletes who use this approach is 11 minutes of running followed by 1 minute of walking. This ratio works very well for many, and since each cycle is 12 minutes, it also divides each hour neatly into five segments (i.e., 5 x 12 minutes = 60 minutes).

- **Avoid Z3 and Above:** The more time we stay below Z3, the stronger our marathon will be. Watch this closely throughout the race. Sure, when you are cycling up a hill, your heart rate may temporarily jump above Z2, but it's important to minimize these occurrences. Keep a close eye on your heart rate and adjust your effort level as needed to maximize your time in the upper half of Z2.

- **Properly Fuel and Hydrate Pre-Race and During the Bike Segment:** If you wait until the marathon to start fueling and hydrating for your marathon, you have waited too long . . . way too long. To run a strong marathon you need to stay well fueled and hydrated pre-race and during the cycling portion, to set up for a strong run. And you then need to continue to fuel and hydrate properly throughout the marathon.

- **Leverage Your Strengths:** Don's strength was his run. Many of his competitors knew this, so they would try to make time on him in the other two sports. He actually used to like this, because he knew that if they overdid it in their stronger sports, their weaker sport, the run, would be even weaker. And if they were able to put a lead on him before the start of the run, they would have to race their marathon knowing that they were not feeling as good as they wanted to, and they also had to deal with the mental pressure that Don was coming.

- **Wear the Proper Shoes:** Many athletes change into the same shoes for an Iron-Distance marathon as they wear for a straight marathon. This may or may not be appropriate. If you wear racing flats or even light trainers for your straight marathons, you may be better off with your regular training shoes for the Iron-Distance marathon, especially if you are not an elite-level competitor. You will be racing longer and your legs will likely already be tired and sore before the Iron-Distance marathon begins. Your regular training shoes are likely to yield the best results.

WHY NOT DO BOTH?

Many of our coached athletes make it their goal to complete both a straight marathon and an Iron-Distance triathlon in the same year. This is a very exciting and motivating goal, and the key to doing both successfully is to space them properly throughout the year. By doing them too closely together, an athlete risks not preparing optimally for both, not being properly rested and re-energized when they need to be, and increasing the risk of injury.

Our suggestion is not to overlap your marathon training program with your Iron-Distance training program. Complete the program for one, have a great race, and then recover and begin the program for the other. A great way that many athletes approach this is to do their marathon in the early spring using one of the sixteen-week programs from this book, and then follow it up with an Iron-Distance triathlon in the fall using one of the programs from our book *Be Iron Fit, 3rd Edition*.

For example, if you select a marathon in April and an Iron-Distance triathlon in November, you can start with one of the sixteen-week marathon training programs in this book around the first of the year to prepare for your April marathon, and then switch to the thirty-week program in *Be Iron Fit* to prepare for your November Iron-Distance triathlon. Wow . . . what a truly amazing year that would be! Not only will this approach help you to accomplish this awesome "double," but it will also allow you to maximize your performance in both races while staying healthy.

We hope this chapter will help you triathletes to improve your marathon performances within the Iron-Distance triathlon, and we hope that we may have inspired many of you to attempt the challenge of a marathon and Iron-Distance triathlon in the same year!

If your goal is to replicate your marathon success in the Iron-Distance triathlon, we hope the tips and information in this chapter will help you to accomplish this truly wonderful goal!

» Summary and Conclusion

Because running fast is more fun than running slow. —FRANK SHORTER

The marathon is an amazing and rewarding challenge and a worthy goal for people of all ages. For some, it's on their "bucket list"—running a marathon is something they want to accomplish as a once-in-a-lifetime experience. For others, it's a lifetime journey that goes far beyond the race itself. Sure, marathoning will always have something to do with improving on your finishing time and competing against yourself. But the journey also involves enjoying a healthy lifestyle, traveling to wonderful places, meeting amazing people, and being part of a very special international community of athletes.

You may be a first-timer after forty years of age, or you may have been racing marathons for so long you have lost count of how many you have completed. One thing is for certain: The training approaches that work for athletes in their teens, twenties, and thirties usually do not work for athletes in their forties, fifties, and sixties. As we mature we need to train smarter and consider new approaches to staying healthy and maximizing the benefits of our training.

Not too long ago, forty was considered by many to be the start of old age, a time when we needed to give up athletics or at least significantly scale back our participation. Athletic competition was for the young. This was believed to be doubly true for something as challenging and physically demanding as a marathon. But not many people feel that way anymore, and there are hundreds of thousands of forty-plus, fifty-plus, and sixty-plus athletes out there getting faster and stronger every year. As this book demonstrates, it is not only possible to continue to train for and participate in marathons after forty, but it's actually possible for many runners to become faster after forty and, most importantly, to enjoy running more than ever.

Along with presenting proven training approaches to help athletes find marathon success over forty, we have also profiled ten successful age-group athletes who became even faster and accomplished even greater performances after the age of forty. By adjusting their approach and training smarter rather than harder, these athletes achieved amazing success after forty, and many of them consistently continue to lower their times, year after year. These are just a sampling of the athletes we have personally had the honor and pleasure to work with. There are thousands and thousands more out there with their own special marathon success stories. If you are not already one of those success stories, we hope that with the help of this book, you will be soon.

Read the entire book before selecting your marathon program. Understand the Three Magic Bullets sessions and how they should be properly complemented with moderate aerobic training sessions and rest days. This is the first major step toward marathon success. Then explore all of the cross-training options, their pros and cons, and determine which are best for you.

Understand the importance of a proper core and functional strength training program combined with the right nutrition to achieve your optimal race weight and maximize your power-to-weight ratio. The program is not only about running and cross-training; it's also about stepping up to the marathon starting line stronger, leaner, and healthier than ever before.

Learn how to avoid and minimize injuries and common training mistakes. Learn how to develop your optimal fueling and hydration plan, along with a proper racing strategy and mental focus techniques for your marathon. All these elements are crucial to your success.

Take all the information in this book; consider your goals, your health history, and your experience level; and then, in consultation with your doctor, select the sixteen-week program that best fits your situation.

Choose a marathon that excites and motivates you and put it on your calendar. There is something amazingly motivating about having a marathon race date on your calendar. You may desire the thrill of a big-city marathon like New York, Chicago, or London, but also consider the hundreds of marathons in smaller cities and towns across North America and the rest of the world. There are so many scenic and challenging races out there in so many wonderful places.

As recommended earlier, don't jump right into the sixteen-week program. Allow at least four to eight weeks of easy running and/or cross-training to gradually build up to the suggested starting level of each program. Then it's all about consistency and training smart. Stick as closely as you can to the program while also training safely and listening carefully to your body. Remember, this is not about "no pain, no gain." You should feel healthy and pain-free throughout the program. If any aches or pains arise, don't wait; seek competent medical advice immediately to head off any potential injury or illness. Good health always comes first.

Review this book frequently throughout the sixteen-week period to remind yourself of each of the tips and suggestions presented and to help keep you motivated and moving forward with a positive mental attitude.

Most importantly, enjoy the journey. Think of every day in the program as a fun challenge, and be thankful that you have the blessings of good health and good fortune to be able to train for and race a marathon. Don't think of your race as simply a goal; think of it as a celebration of an incredible journey.

» APPENDIX A: SUGGESTED READING

The books listed here have been very helpful to us over the years and provided us with a great deal of information as we compiled our research for this book. They may prove useful to you as well.

Advanced Marathoning. 2nd ed. Pete Pfitzinger and Scott Douglas. Human Kinetics, 2009.

Body, Mind and Sport: The Mind-Body Guide to Lifelong Fitness and Your Personal Best. John Douillard. Crown Trade Paperbacks, 1994.

Core Performance: The Revolutionary Workout Program to Transform Your Body and Your Life. Mark Verstegen and Pete Williams. Rodale Inc., 2004.

The Core Program: Fifteen Minutes a Day That Can Change Your Life. Peggy Brill and Gerald Secor Couzens. Bantam, 2003.

Eating for Endurance. Dr. Philip Maffetone. David Barmore Productions, 1999.

Galloway's Book on Running. Jeff Galloway. Shelter Publications, 2002.

How to Eat, Move and Be Healthy! Paul Chek. C.H.E.K. Institute Publishing, 2004.

The Inner Athlete: Realizing Your Fullest Potential. Dan Millman. Stillpoint Publishing, 1994.

Instant Relief: Tell Me Where It Hurts and I'll Tell You What to Do. Peggy Brill and Susan Suffes. Bantam, 2007.

Lifestyle & Weight Management Consultant Manual. Richard T. Cotton. American Council on Exercise, 1996.

The Marathon Method. The 16-Week Training Program That Prepares You to Finish a Full or Half Marathon in Your Best Time. Tom Holland. Fair Winds Press, 2007.

Marathon: The Ultimate Training Guide, 3rd ed. Hal Higdon. Rodale Inc., 2005.

Masters Running: A Guide to Running and Staying Fit after 40. Hal Higdon. Rodale Inc., 2005.

The Non-Runner's Marathon Trainer. David A. Whitsett, Forrest A. Dolgener, and Tanjala Mabon Kole. McGraw Hill, 1998.

Personal Trainer Manual—The Resource for Fitness Professionals. Richard T. Cotton. American Council on Exercise, 1997.

Program Design for Personal Trainers: Bridging Theory into Application. Douglas S. Brooks, MS. Human Kinetics, 1997.

Run Faster from the 5K to the Marathon: How to Be Your Own Best Coach. Brad Hudson and Matt Fitzgerald. Broadway, 2008.

Runner's World, Run Less Run Faster: Become a Faster, Stronger Runner with the Revolutionary FIRST Training Program. Bill Pierce, Scott Murr, and Ray Moss. Rodale Inc., 2007.

Serious Training For Endurance Athletes. Rob Sleamaker and Ray Browning. Human Kinetics, 1996.

Training Lactate Pulse-Rate. Peter G. J. M. Janssen. Polar Electro Oy, 1987.

» APPENDIX B: SUGGESTED WEBSITES

Australia Marathons: Runcalendar.com.au

Half Marathon Guide: www.halfmarathons.net

IronFit: www.ironfit.com

Marathon Canada: www.marathoncanada.com

Marathon Guide: www.marathonguide.com

Marathons in New Zealand: www.runningcalendar.co.nz

Run Britain: www.runbritain.com

Runner's World: www.runnersworld.com

South America Marathon Calendar: http://marathons.ahotu.com/calendar/marathon/south-america

» APPENDIX C: GLOSSARY

Active Recovery: Lower-intensity running or cross-training sessions that allow the body to recover while continuing to build and/or maintain fitness.

Aerobic Energy System: An energy system that utilizes oxygen and stored fat to power muscle activity. This system can support activity for prolonged periods of time, as stored fat and oxygen are available in almost endless supply.

Anaerobic Energy System: An energy system that utilizes glycogen (stored sugar) to power muscle activity. This system cannot support activity for long periods of time, as the body stores sugar in relatively limited quantities.

Banking Time: Racing the first part of the marathon at a significantly faster pace than the athlete's Target Marathon Pace in an effort to accumulate extra time to help achieve the athlete's marathon time goal.

Carbohydrate Loading (aka "carbo-loading"): Various dietary approaches for the purpose of increasing glycogen stores prior to an endurance race.

Cooldown: Lower-intensity activity after training or racing to help the body to gradually prepare itself to stop or greatly reduce its level of physical activity.

Cross-training: Training activities other than actual running that are good substitutes for actual running.

Free Miles Training Hierarchy: A scale used to determine whether an athlete is able to do all his training or only a small amount of his training in the form of running.

Free Running Miles: Cross-training activities that provide similar benefits to actual running, but do not carry some of the negative risks of running (e.g., high impact).

Glycogen: The form in which the body stores sugar for the purpose of powering muscle activity.

Half Marathon Training Program: A specific multiweek training plan designed to prepare an athlete to run a half marathon. The authors present several twelve-week half marathon training programs in this book.

Heart Rate Zones: Heart-rate ranges expressed in terms of beats per minute (BPM) that correspond to the intensity levels of physical activities.

Higher-Intensity Inserts: A single higher-intensity portion within a moderate run session, usually between 5 and 15 minutes in duration.

Higher-Intensity Repeats: This is one of the Three Magic Bullets sessions (TMBs). It includes several consecutive higher-intensity portions, separated by easy jogs in between. The higher-intensity portions are usually completed at a pace of at least 30 seconds per mile faster than Target Marathon Pace.

Hill Repeats: This session is similar to Higher-Intensity Repeats. It includes several consecutive higher-intensity runs up a hill, separated by easy jogs back down the hill to the starting point.

Lactate Threshold: The heart-rate level at which lactate begins to accumulate at a faster rate in the muscles than the body can clear it. Lactate is produced in our bodies when performing physical activity. The accumulation of lactate has a negative impact on the muscles' ability to perform.

Long Run: This is one of the Three Magic Bullets sessions (TMBs). It is the longest run of the week and is typically completed at a pace equal to 30 to 60 seconds slower than Target Marathon Pace.

Marathon Pacing Session (MPS): This is one of the Three Magic Bullets sessions (TMBs). It is a run session that includes an insert portion at the athlete's Target Marathon Pace.

Marathon Time Goal: The specific time in which the athlete wants to complete the marathon (e.g., 3 hours and 30 minutes).

Marathon Training Program: A specific multiweek training plan designed to prepare an athlete to run a marathon. The authors present several sixteen-week Marathon Training Programs in this book.

Maximum Heart Rate (MHR): The highest heart rate attainable by a specific athlete, expressed in terms of beats per minute (BPM).

Negative Splitting: Running later segments of a race increasingly faster than the previous segments. For example, running the second half of a marathon faster than the first half.

Rest Days: Days on which the athlete does no training activity at all, for the purpose of allowing his body to recover.

Sweat-Rate Test: A test to help an athlete determine the quantity of his perspiration over a given time period and under certain conditions.

Taper: A training period prior to a race in which the athlete does progressively less and less training volume as the race approaches. The purpose is to become fully rested before the race, without losing fitness.

Target Marathon Pace: This is the pace at which the athlete plans to attempt to run in his next marathon. This pace is usually expressed in terms of minutes per mile.

Three Magic Bullets (TMBs): The three most important weekly training sessions of a successful marathon training plan. They are the Higher-Intensity Repeats, Marathon Pacing Session, and Long Run.

Training Race: A specific race included in a Marathon Training Program for the purpose of preparing the athlete to achieve his marathon time goal.

Training Volume: The combination of how long you run, how intense your effort level is while you run, and how frequently you run. Training volume can be expressed by the following equation: Training Volume – Duration x Intensity x Frequency.

Transition Sessions (aka "brick sessions"): A training session in which a cross training activity is combined with actual running. For example: The athlete completes a 45-minute bike ride and then immediately follows it up with a 15-minute run.

Warm-up: Lower-intensity activity before training or racing to help the body gradually prepare itself for a higher level of physical activity.

»ACKNOWLEDGMENTS

We wish to thank the following individuals: Steve Adler, Jodi Lee Alper, Joe Altomare, Martin Avidan, Tim Beasant, Jonathan Beverly, M. Scott Boyles, Peggy Brill, Kellie Brown, Tracie Brown, Bill Christian, Sorin Ciocan, Carl Curran, David Drucker, Gary Gluzman, Stephen Grossman, Craig and Brenda Gruber, Holt Harrell, Yvonne Hernandez, Peter Hyland, Lynn Kellogg, Nick King, Stephen Levine, Jeff Liccardi, Michael Lish, Laura Litwin, Dave Mantle, Ed McEntee, James Mitchell, Ric Mora, Adrianna Nelson, Nuta Olaru, Soula Privolos, Francis Quinn, Melissa and Cary Silverman, Aya Stevens, Kevin Stevens, Hugh Temple, and Debra Trebitz.

»INDEX

» ABOUT THE AUTHORS

Don Fink is an internationally known triathlon and running coach/trainer and author of the popular endurance sports training books *Be IronFit: Time-Efficient Training Secrets for Ultimate Fitness* (3rd edition, 2015), *IronFit Triathlon Training for Women* (2014), *IronFit Strength Training and Nutrition for Endurance Athletes* (2013), and *IronFit Secrets for Half Iron-Distance Triathlon Success* (2013), all published by Lyons Press. Among his credentials, Don is a certified personal trainer through the American Council on Exercise (ACE) and a professional member of the National Strength and Conditioning Association. Don and Melanie train endurance athletes on five continents through their business, IronFit (ironfit.com). Don and Melanie have utilized their innovative approaches to coach hundreds of athletes to personal best times and breakthrough performances in the marathon, half marathon, ultras, triathlon, and other sports.

Melanie Fink, Don Fink, and Sheena
Lynn Kellogg/www.trilifephotos.com

In addition to being an endurance sports coach/trainer, Don is an elite athlete. He has raced more than thirty Iron-Distance triathlons (2.4-mile swim, 112-mile bike, and 26.2-mile run) and has many age-group victories and course records to his credit. Don's time of 9:08 at the 2004 Ironman Florida is still one of the fastest times recorded by an athlete in the 45–49 age group.

Don also placed in the top three overall in the 2002 Ultraman World Championships (6.2-mile swim, 262-mile bike, and 52.4-mile run) on the Big Island of Hawaii.

Melanie is a certified personal trainer and health coach through ACE and a six-year past Regional Council member of USAT Triathlon Mid-Atlantic. She coauthored all of the books mentioned above.

In addition to being an endurance sports coach/trainer and Level 2 Masters Swimming coach, Melanie is an elite athlete as well. She has many age-group and overall victories in triathlon and open water swimming competitions, has completed twelve Iron-Distance triathlons (including the Hawaii Ironman twice), and completed Ultraman Canada (6.2-mile swim, 270-mile bike, 52.4-mile run) in Penticton, British Columbia. Melanie's passion is helping athletes at all levels to get into running and endurance sports and to become athletes for life.

Don and Melanie live in Carroll County, New Hampshire.